The Quest for World Order

Michigan Faculty Series

The Quest for World Order

Robert Cooley Angell

Ann Arbor   The University of Michigan Press

Library of Congress Cataloging in Publication Data

Angell, Robert Cooley, 1899-
    The quest for world order.

    (Michigan faculty series)
    Includes bibliographical references and index.
    1.   World politics —1945-   2.   United
Nations.   I.   Title.
D843.A523   1978   327'.09'04   78-14248
ISBN 0-472-06304-9

To our grandchildren

Acknowledgments

I am happy to express my thanks to the following scholars for their generous assistance at various points in the preparation of this study: Professor Jacques Freymond and Dr. Antoine Fleury of the Graduate Institute of International Studies at Geneva; Professor Dusan Sidjanski of the University of Geneva; Professor Stein Rokkan, Director of the Chr. Michelsen Institute at Bergen; Drs. Helge Hveem and Kjell Skjelsbaek of the Peace Research Institute, Oslo; Dr. Alva Myrdal, former Swedish Ambassador to India; Ms. Cecilia Molander of the Swedish Institute of International Affairs; Professor M. Donald Hancock of the University of Texas at Austin; and Professor Thomas Anton of the University of Michigan.

Contents

1. The Threatening Crisis   1
2. Nationalism   9
3. National Support for World Order   15
4. The Pioneers   33
5. Who Will Follow the Pioneers?   57
6. The United Nations   81
7. Regional Intergovernmental Organizations   113
8. The Web of International Nongovernmental   127
   Relations
9. Call for Global Effort   149

Appendices
   A. Allocation of Causal Influence to the Predictors   161
   B. Predicted Scores on the Index of National Support
        for World Order of 114 Nations   163
   C. Limitations on Organizations Selected for
        Study of Bridging   165
   D. Members of Mutual Security Organizations   166

   Notes   169
   Index   177

Tables

1. Scores of 114 Nations on the Index of National   19
   Support for World Order
2. Correlations of the Predictors with the Seven   26
   Separate Indicators and with the NSWO Index
3. Percentages of Influence Allocated to Five   29
   Predictors
4. Potentiality for Enlightened Patriotism of   59
   Thirty-eight Nations
5. Revised Estimates of Potentiality for Enlightened   79
   Patriotism of Twenty Nations
6. Diplomatic Experience at the U.N. Compared   83
   with a National Capital
7. Convergence of Scientific and Technical Culture   145
   as Shown by INGO Memberships
8. Convergence of Global Values as Shown by   146
   INGO Memberships
9. Relations between Predictors and the NSWO   162
   Index

1
The Threatening Crisis

Balance-of-power diplomacy among the great European states managed to produce some order in world affairs during the nineteenth century. With the outbreak of World War I in 1914, that order virtually disappeared for three decades. Since 1945 humanity has been floundering, seeking a new equilibrium in a world of nuclear weapons, ideological conflict, and decolonization. At the close of World War II there were high hopes that the United Nations could create a stable world. These hopes were disappointed by the onset of the Cold War between the Communist and Western blocs; but hopes sprang up again when the United States and the Soviet Union began, in 1969, to discuss a Strategic Arms Limitation Treaty and, with the signing in 1972 of the first SALT agreement, embraced détente. Although six years have since passed without any reversal of the arms race, it is expected that an agreement will be reached in early 1979 to impose minor restrictions in several categories of weapons. Even if this happens, it will be only a modest step toward disarmament.

Some students of world affairs, however, are optimistic that the crying need for world order will compel a movement to achieve it. Robert E. Heilbroner is one who does not agree. In his impressive study, *Inquiry into the Human Prospect*, he takes a gloomy view indeed.[1] Among the specters he glimpses are (1) a rate of population growth that either impoverishes much of the developing world, with consequent famine, pillage, and riots, or gives rise to authoritarian governments that bring a coercive halt to population growth; (2) a competition among nations for resources so sharp as to provoke the seizure of territory by the powerful from the powerless, the outbreak of nuclear wars among the powerful, or the blackmail of the powerful by poor nations possessed of nuclear arms; and (3) a decline in industrial output from exhaustion of energy resources and deterioration of the biosphere though pollution. He concludes: "If, then, by the question 'Is there hope for man?' we ask whether it is possible to meet the challenges of the future without the payment of a fearful price, the answer must be: No, there is no such hope."[2]

Heilbroner is no impulsive Cassandra. His book was published two decades after experts had warned of the ominous consequences of the population explosion following World War II and the dangers of radioactive fallout from weapons tests and reactor malfunctions. In 1962, Rachel Carson's *Silent Spring* awakened the world to the degradation of the environment through man's irresponsible use of herbicides and pesticides and his industrial pollution.[3] The public did not become aware of the imminent scarcity of many industrial metals until the sixties, nor the dangerous rate at which oil and gas reserves were being depleted until the seventies. All of these threats were exposed in 1972 in the first report to the Club of Rome, the computerized projection of trends entitled *The Limits to Growth*,[4] but they had been dealt with less elaborately by Richard A. Falk in *This Endangered Planet* the year before.[5] Just after the appearance of Heilbroner's book came the second report to the Club of Rome, *Mankind at the Turning Point* by Mihajlo Mesarovic and Eduard Pestel, which used computer analysis to portray alternative possibilities between 1975 and 2025 in ten world regions.[6] Here the message came through clearly that, even if there were efficient operation now of a well-conceived world plan, the time would be already late. A few bad harvests could condemn millions to starvation within a decade and, if by that time a multifaceted program to meet the most pressing problems were not going forward, such dismal consequences as foreseen by Heilbroner would ensue.

The second report to the Club of Rome recognizes the urgent need for cooperation among nations if any global program is to be conceived and carried through successfully.

> Cooperation is no longer a schoolroom word suggesting an ethical but elusive mode of behavior; cooperation is a scientifically supported, politically viable, and absolutely essential mode of behavior for the organic growth of the world system. . . . Cooperation connotes interdependence. Increasing interdependence between nations and regions must then translate as a decrease in independence. Nations cannot be interdependent without each of them giving up some of, or at least acknowledging limits to, its own independence.[7]

And again:

> The futility of narrow nationalism must be appreciated and taken as an axiom in the decision-making framework. Global issues can be solved only by global concerted action.[8]

Hard as *Mankind at the Turning Point* bears down on this point, there is no discussion of how this change in sentiment from nationalism to humanism is to come about. In a commentary at the end of the volume, Aurelio Peccei and Alexander King, speaking for the Club of Rome, say only: "Yet we are moderately hopeful. The winds of change have begun to blow. A keen and anxious awareness is evolving to suggest that fundamental changes will have to take place in the world order and its power structures, in the distribution of wealth and income, in our outlook and behavior."[9] A few scientists may be aware that fundamental changes will have to take place, but there is as yet no canvass of the possible ways in which that awareness could become general and crystallized into global plans and programs of action.

There is a further serious obstacle that is not mentioned in either the first or second report to the Club of Rome and is little discussed in other writings on world problems. This is the fact that incompatible sentiments of justice are often involved in attempts to solve these problems. For example, the developing countries feel that they were exploited for generations by their colonial masters and that they are still exploited in a sort of neocolonialism by the operation of multinational corporations based in the developed countries. They feel that any plan for the allocation of resources among the peoples of the world should compensate them for that exploitation. Many groups in the developed countries, on the other hand, feel it equitable that these new nations raise themselves by their own bootstraps, as did the European industrial countries in the nineteenth century. Thus, solutions to problems are going to require not only agreement on what needs to be done technically, but agreement on how benefits and costs are to be distributed.

On an even broader scale, value changes are imperative if Heilbroner's scenario is not to become a reality. If catastrophe is to be avoided, there must be greater concern for future generations as compared with generations now alive, and greater concern for humanity as a whole as compared with one's own nation. The two values that have to be modified— exclusive concern for present welfare and narrow nationalism—are deeply seated and will not yield to purely rational argument. The necessity of these two changes, long apparent, has been acknowledged in two later reports to the Club of Rome, *Reshaping the International Order* and *Goals for Mankind*.[10]

The present situation comes down to this, then. What has been written since 1960 has shocked the sophisticated public into a realization of the dire probabilities ahead and has presented in increasing detail the complexities and interrelations of the problems. Although these writings have brought enlightenment to what needs to be done on the physical and biological side, they have shed little light on how to foster the necessary cooperation between nations. Nor have political scientists been of great help. For the most part they have clung to the traditional view of the world that sees the principal actors as sovereign states pursuing their national interests in competition and, often, in conflict. This is the view that has brought the world to its present dangerous state and that underlies Heilbroner's pessimistic prophecy.

It would be an error, however, to conclude that there has been no movement toward tackling global problems. There is a gradual spreading of awareness among the well educated that these problems must be approached from a world, not a national, perspective. The first step in solving any problem, however, is to grasp its seriousness. Thanks to writers like Rachel Carson, Richard Falk, and Robert Heilbroner, and to organizations like the Club of Rome, that seriousness is becoming widely appreciated. Concerted efforts are already being made to abate pollution, control population growth, harness solar energy, develop aquaculture, and shift to the utilization of renewable resources. Disarmament negotiations continue and possible ways of allocating the world's energy and mineral resources are under study. Given two or three decades, humanity would probably be able to meet the multifold challenge if the globe were ruled by a philosopher-king, but such a ruler's appearance is extremely unlikely. There is grave doubt that humanity can bring its discordant elements together sufficiently to falsify Heilbroner's prophecy. In short, there is a fateful race going on between forces striving for world consensus and the accumulation of frictions that could ultimately generate a nuclear war.

World order is the polar opposite of what Heilbroner foresees. However vague this concept, it is clear that we do not have what it suggests. Despite the elaborate system of diplomacy among nations, despite the network of treaties, despite the United Nations and its many specialized agencies, animosities between nations remain too deep seated, fears of aggression too constant, and wars too frequent. Each nation insists upon complete freedom of action. The ultimate objective is the welfare and power of its own people. In a time of crisis, con-

cern for other peoples or even for humanity as a whole fades
into the background. The policy adopted is narrow and self-
serving. In the past, humanity could suffer this degree of
world anarchy (if not with equanimity, at least without fear of
universal annihilation). Those days are gone. The stockpiles of
nuclear weapons having unimaginable destructive power have
made the attainment of world order mandatory. A great
atomic physicist put it bluntly thirty years ago:

> It is a practical thing to recognize as a common respon-
> sibility, wholly incapable of unilateral solution, the com-
> plete common peril that atomic weapons constitute for
> the world, to recognize that only by a community of
> responsibility is there any hope of meeting the peril.[11]

It is clear that the present system is too weak. Since World
War II it has been incapable of keeping the peace in Asia,
Africa, and the Middle East. A tempting solution would be for
the nuclear powers to reach an agreement on the most effective way of ruling the globe and to impose their will on the
other states, perhaps dividing the world into spheres of influence. They might even promise, at later stages, to democratize
relations within each sphere and then to federate the spheres
into a world state.

This solution seems unfeasible because the ex-colonial states
have, for the first time, tested the heady wine of power. After
they have cast votes in the United Nations, any attempt to
subjugate them again would be a bloody business. Nor is the
establishment of a universal state feasible. Though one can
imagine all the peoples of the world jointly forming a confederation and bringing their sovereignties together into a
functioning union, this is surely, for decades to come, a vision-
ary project. Its success would be so doubtful that few large
states would give up their independent military power for the
chancy benefits of a world government.[12] Two economists
have expressed their skepticism: "The nation-state may all too

seldom speak the voice of reason. But it remains the only serious alternative to chaos."[13]

Thus there are severe limitations on the structure of any world order that could conceivably be realized before the year 2000. The task of projecting a scheme that might work satisfactorily would daunt the most confident futurist. The world order must be stronger than that achieved by the United Nations; it cannot soon, if ever, be a world state; and it will have to be acceptable to most nations. These prescriptions do not allow much latitude. Clearly, cooperation among nations must be achieved and armaments reduced by new processes of consultation, negotiation, and persuasion. The institutional arrangements that would foster these processes are presently unknown. It is possible that the very urgency of problems like famine, the population explosion, pollution, and scarcity of resources will so deepen the sense of crisis as to produce consensus on unprecedented measures. Perhaps regional organizations will gradually grow stronger, allowing the United Nations the opportunity to intensify its attention to global problems.

Despite the dangers that humanity faces and the uncertainties of how to cope with them, men and women are not likely to despair. They will try to meet the challenge without paying Heilbroner's "fearful price" of world catastrophe. It becomes imperative, therefore, to canvass possible developments that might avert the tragedy. This is the agenda of the present study.

Such an agenda could be endless in so complicated a world, however, if there were not some guideline for the canvass. This I have found in the thought of my sociological mentor, Charles Horton Cooley, who sixty years ago set forth his theory of the tentative process.[14] He believed that societies and their institutions, like persons and groups, adapt to their physical and social surroundings tentatively, by trial and error. The innovations tried are selected or discarded depending on whether they "work." Those that satisfy the dominant needs of the society or institution survive and are built upon; the rest fade away.

Employing Cooley's conception of social process, I have searched for developments on the world scene that are relevant to the establishment of world order. I have tried to estimate their degree of tentative success or failure and thus get some glimpse of future prospects. Since modern communications and air transportation have made for increasing connections among peoples and nations, it is very probable that these new linkages have stimulated adjustive reactions and initiatives. I have seen my task, then, as probing these tentative moves to discover whether any of them are showing promise of inching the world toward greater order and justice.

2
Nationalism

A great general learns as much as possible about the personal characteristics and the tactical style of the opposing commander before he sends his men into battle. Since it is nationalism that stands as the chief obstacle to achieving the cooperation that would solve global problems, it is prudent to understand its characteristics before seeking ways to counter it.

Since the French Revolution, nationalism has been recognized as Janus-faced. It promotes unity, loyalty, and order among the citizens of a country, but it also makes for suspicion, intolerance, and conflict between countries. Although it is rarely the sole cause of war, nationalism exacerbates disputes and frequently makes them impossible to settle by negotiation and compromise. After pointing out that nationalism is usually the enemy of peace, Gunnar Myrdal writes:

> ... Irrational nationalism of governments and, behind them, of peoples is demonstrated in the present relative lack of willingness to come to agreements on mutual settlements in the wider range of economic, social, and legal international disputes. Leaving such issues unsettled, or not well settled, is on the one hand, caused by narrow nationalistic attitudes of governments, ordinarily

supported by their nations. On the other hand, it tends, in turn, to feed nationalism in all countries, and then, in the extreme case, to make them prepared to break the peace.[1]

Myrdal's testimony, like that of many others, brings out the need to understand nationalism thoroughly before seeking antidotes for it.

To understand nationalism requires a prior grasp of the concepts state and nationality. The state is the institution that, acting through government, exercises ultimate control over the people occupying a territory. A nationality is a group of people sharing enough common culture to have strong fellow feeling and to identify themselves as different from others. Nationalism is the doctrine, the aspiration, and the movement that seeks to achieve and maintain for a nationality its own state. In short, nationalism is a nationality's propensity for self-government. Its natural expression is "we" as against the rest of the world. It expresses a grievance against foreigners. Where a nationality is a minority in a state that it does not dominate, it usually wants to secede and, if that is impossible, it often rebels. Rebellion is particularly likely if members of the same nationality control a contiguous state that could come to the aid of the rebels.

Scholars differ on when nationalism first reared its head, but all agree that it originated in Western Europe and that by the eighteenth century it was clearly in evidence. The faith of the Enlightenment in human reason gave support to nationalism's approval of popular, as opposed to dynastic, sovereignty. The ethnic group, with its common culture, replaced the dynasty. The American and French revolutions are regarded as early expressions of nationalism. During the nineteenth century, country after country in Europe felt the movement's impact and revised its political system to give nationalism expression. The Latin American countries did likewise. In the twentieth century, as levels of education rose and colonies declared their

independence from imperial powers, the nationalistic movement spread to Asia and Africa.

The term nation implies that a nationality has found expression in a state. This can come about in three ways. A
preexistent nationality may achieve its own state, as did the
German nationality in 1871 and the Polish nationality at the
end of World War I. Or, a preexistent state may generate a new
nationality from within, through the long interaction of the
people on its territory. This is exemplified by the history of
Switzerland. The third route to nationhood is through rebellion of a colony, with both a sense of nationality and a new
state developing together. This seems to have happened with
the birth of the United States.

There has been serious difficulty with the concept of nation,
however. The citizens of a state are rarely members of a single
nationality—Icelands and Norways are few. The fact is that the
nation is an "ideal type," an abstract embodiment of what is
only a tendency for political communities to coincide with
sociocultural communities. When cultural minorities are
small, the usual assumption has been that, in time, they would
be assimilated into the dominant nationality. This ·has occurred in the United States with immigrants of European
nationalities, but only partially with American Indian and
black minorities. Other minorities that have not been well
assimilated are the Bretons in France, the Austrians of the
South Tyrol in Italy, and the Basques and Catalans in Spain.
When minorities are numerous, the expectation has often been
that a new, broad nationality would develop and supersede the
older majority and minority nationalities. The Soviet Union
includes fourteen republics, each expressing a different nationality, and Yugoslavia includes Croat, Slovene, Serb, and
Macedonian nationalities. There seems to have evolved more
of an overarching sense of nationality in the Soviet case than in
the Yugoslav one, but in neither case is the concept of the
nation fully realized. In Belgium, surprisingly, what was once a
firm Belgian nationality seems to be breaking down into its

constituent Flemish and Walloon parts. Finally, there is many a new state in Africa in which a leader hopes to create a new nationality to supersede the traditional tribes.

Instances such as these lead naturally to two questions: (1) In speaking of all the political units in the world should we give up calling them nations? and (2) Has the power of nationalism in the world been exaggerated?

The alternatives to nation as a general term are country and state. Neither of these would call attention to the powerful political influence of nationalism over the last two centuries. Even where a true nation has not been achieved, it is an objective; hence the influence of nationalism is present. In the attempt to recognize the different patterns of relation between state and nationality, scholars have used two terms, nation-state and state-nation. The first term is used when a single nationality dominates the state; the second is used when such dominance is an unrealized aspiration and the state itself is the principal unifying influence. The difficulty with these designations is that the assignment to one or the other category has to be arbitrary. If we take as a standard that 85 percent of the population of a country has to be of a single nationality for it to qualify as a nation-state, then, according to the *Encyclopedia Britannica*, 54 of 115 countries for which nationality proportions are specified are nation-states. Most of the remainder are presumably state-nations. Different cutoff points, say 75 percent or 90 percent, would increase or decrease the number of nation-states. The unlikelihood of consensus among scholars on a single cutoff point, or on any other method of division, makes this solution unpromising. It seems wise, therefore, to retain nation as a general term for nation-states and state-nations, and to use the two subordinate terms to mark a qualitative distinction, not as labels for definite categories.

The second query raises the issue of whether nationalism has ebbed with the virtual end of colonialism and the creation of many new, independent states. In the recent past, there is no doubt that the nationalism of the major states was the greatest obstacle to world order. Each wanted to achieve and maintain a position of power that would give effect to its national policies. In its crudest form, a nationalistic state has aimed to dominate the other states in its orbit of contact. In a more sophisticated form, it has aimed to secure at least equal dignity for itself in a context of nationalistic states. In both cases it has rejected external control, insisting that its worth requires self-determination on all vital issues. Thus, nationalism has made for incompatible views among countries on many global problems.

But what of the present situation? The fact that 54 of the 115 nations discussed qualify as nation-states under the 85 percent standard testifies to the continuing significance of nationality within states. These 54 have 51 percent of the population of the 115 nations and 68 percent of their gross national product. Thus each of the nation-states has, on the average, 2.4 times the economic power of each of the 61 remaining countries. Even this comparison does not do justice to the power of nationalism. Its spirit is strong in many countries like the Soviet Union, India, and Britain that do not qualify as nation-states under the 85 percent standard.

This is not to say that nationalism is always chauvinistic. There seems to be a process of maturation similar to that widely noticed in religious movements. Sociologists have distinguished between the sect and the church. The sect is usually a group of ardent believers in a new religious doctrine. The members are clannish, distrustful of outsiders, and confident in the superiority of their creed and way of life. The church, on the other hand, has evolved from the sect by adjusting to the surrounding society. It is less doctrinaire than the sect and less distrustful of outsiders. A similar comparison can be made between a nationality aspiring to possess its own state and a mature nation. During the struggle to achieve recognition in a state, the people are enthusiastic, united, and loyal to the cause. Once their nationality dominates a state recognized by the world as legitimate, secular routine gradually sets in, enthusiasm wanes somewhat, and nationalism moderates. The more the nation settles down and accommodates to the realities of its life in the world of nations, the less chauvinistic is likely to be its temper. One can perhaps rightly say that Germany regressed to immaturity under Hitler.

It is more difficult to make any generalization about state-nations like Nigeria or Yugoslavia. Since they are not characterized by strong national sentiment, they lack a strong sense of unity, making their course of development less predictable than that of nation-states. They may in time become nationalistic, but this is not at all certain; they may remain unified by the pragmatic advantages of economic and political order; or, they may even fail as states, torn apart by conflicting loyalties. Their relations to neighboring states, like the course of their domestic affairs, is unpredictable.

There is no doubt that disillusion with nationalism has been mounting during the last half century. Morris Ginsberg gives four persuasive reasons. The first is the world-wide disappointment with the aggressive nationalism shown by the Germans, the Italians, and the Japanese in World War II. A second is the disappointment with the consequences of the Wilsonian insistence on the recognition of nationalities in the Treaty of Versailles at the conclusion of World War I. As a result there has developed, thirdly, a conviction that small national states are not viable, become danger spots, and tempt larger states to conquest. Finally, there has been a growing realization that wider forms of political organization than that represented in nations are necessary in the modern world.[2]

There is, however, a countertrend. The ex-colonial nations are now cultivating a nationalistic spirit as a means of uniting their constituent tribes. They are in somewhat the situation of the European powers two centuries ago. Another stimulant to nationalism is the desire of the Communist satellites in Eastern Europe to lessen the dominance of the Soviet Union over their economic and political destinies.

There seems to be, then, no worldwide tendency in respect to nationalism. It is under criticism in some quarters and striven for in others, but there is no doubt that in its varied guises nationalism is highly relevant to the quest for world order.

3
National Support for World Order

Since nations are the most autonomous units in the field of international relations, it seems appropriate to apply first to them the concept of the tentative process. How are they evolving in response to contemporary conditions? Is increasing interconnection between nations eliciting initiatives toward world order?

In 1969 I undertook a study of national support for world order from this standpoint. I hoped that I would find marked differences between nations on such support and that I could then discover differences in background conditions that would explain them.[1] These explanations would be of help to anyone trying to design a strategy for world peace. A full technical account of that study has been published elsewhere.[2] Here I shall discuss its essentials, with as little professional jargon as possible. Since, however, the results of this study are the foundation for the analysis in this and the next chapter of the contributions, actual and potential, of various nations to a firmer world order, I am obligated to make the presentation thorough.

It seemed wise to measure support for world order by using several indicators that could later be combined into an index yielding a single score for each nation. The basic concept is a broad one, involving both attitude and action, and is likely to show itself in several specific ways. The search for appropriate

15

indicators was difficult, since they had to be ones for which data were available for most nations of the world. Seven indicators out of a large number given serious consideration were finally chosen. The data on which scores for each nation were based come from the period 1960–69.

Since the United Nations and the U.N. Specialized Agencies form the dominant network through which governments try to carry out global tasks collectively, four of the seven indicators used related to that system. The first, called contributions/assessments, aims to measure the commitment of each nation. It does so by comparing the assessments for eight years to the United Nations and seven specialized agencies (each assessment proportional to the nation's capacity to pay) with the voluntary contributions made to United Nations projects not covered by the assessments. The larger the ratio of such voluntary contributions to the assessments, the greater the commitment.[3]

The second indicator aims to measure the conscientiousness with which governments perform their U.N. duties. It is called absences and abstentions and was based on roll call votes in the U.N. General Assembly over eight years. For absences, the rationale is that the less the attendance, the less support for world order. For abstentions, I decided that some of them are statesmanlike acts expressing unwillingness to embrace either horn of an unwisely posed dilemma. After analysis of the data, I concluded that about 15 percent of the abstentions were of this sort. The greater the deviation of a country from that figure, either above or below it, the less the support for world order. The proportion of absences was combined with the scores on abstentions to generate the value of the indicator for each nation.

The size of a nation's delegation to the United Nations as compared with the average size of its embassies abroad constitutes the third indicator, called diplomatic representation.[4] The assumption is that the countries that give higher priority than others to world order will assign a greater proportion of their diplomatic personnel to the United Nations headquarters.

The fourth indicator, bilateral treaty references, has a more indirect relation to the United Nations than does financial commitment, voting responsibility, or diplomatic representation. It expresses the frequency with which a nation agrees to use United Nations agencies in giving effect to its bilateral treaties with other nations. The ratio used is the number of references to such agencies divided by the number of treaties.[5] The rationale, here, is that the more countries use the United Nations as an instrument in their relations with one another, the more support they are giving to world order.

There were three indicators of support for world order unrelated to the United Nations. One of these, the fifth in all, is labeled cooperation/conflict. The assumption was that nations whose governments are cooperative with each other are supporting world order. The data represent careful coding of articles in all copies of *The New York Times* from January 1966 through August 1969.[6]

The sixth indicator consists of the contributions of the government and people of each nation to the International Committee of the Red Cross and associated organizations (1963–69), divided by the nation's gross national product. Since the contributions of governments greatly exceeded those of private citizens and groups, I thought it proper to use this indicator as one of the seven that measure governmental support for world order. Switzerland has much the highest ratio of contribution to gross national product, presumably because the International Committee of the Red Cross is a Swiss corporation.

The final indicator was called IGO memberships and attempted to express the national support for intergovernmental organizations outside the United Nations family. A review of all such organizations in the 1966-67 edition of the *Yearbook of International Organizations* revealed that only five had more than sixty members each. These organizations were potentially universal in the sense that they had no regional, religious, ideological, or ethnic base, and that their objectives were such as to be potentially of interest to all countries.[7]

The seven indicators of national support for world order all reflect the attitudes and actions of governments, whether through the United Nations or not. Readers who condemn all government as "the establishment" will reject these indicators as representative of the people's orientation toward world order. In defense of my procedures, I would claim that governments are currently the effective actors for nations in the world arena. The positions they take are what predominantly influence other nations.

The 114 nations that could be scored on five or more of the seven indicators were included in the study. Of these, four were not then members of the United Nations and do not, therefore, have scores on absences and abstentions. They have contributions/assessments scores, however, because they belong to specialized agencies of the U.N. All 114 nations have scores on IGO memberships also. Mongolia has no score on Red Cross contributions because its gross national product for 1965 was unknown. For want of necessary data, there were only 100 nations with scores on diplomatic representation, and 88 with scores on cooperation/conflict. Because nations with fewer than ten treaties recorded were omitted, there were only 94 nations scored on bilateral treaty references. The well-known nations that could not be scored on five indicators were the People's Republic of China, the People's Republic of Korea, the Democratic Republic of Vietnam, the Democratic Republic of Germany, Rhodesia, Burundi, Singapore, and Trinidad and Tobago.

The several scores for each nation were combined into a single index of support for world order (the NSWO index) by averaging the standardized scores on the several indicators. The NSWO scores for the 114 nations are given in table 1. Because of the manner of computation, for all practical purposes a score of eighty would equal 100 percent on an ordinary scale and a score of twenty would equal 0. The proportions between high and low scores in the original data are not preserved. Thus, a score of seventy would not represent twice as much national support for world order as a score of thirty five.

TABLE 1

Scores of 114 Nations on the Index of National
Support for World Order

Rank	Nation	Score	Rank	Nation	Score
1	Switzerland	73.47		Italy	53.56
	Denmark	63.96		Iraq	53.54
	Sweden	62.92			
	Norway	62.04	26	Greece	53.15
	Kuwait	59.23		Iceland	52.95
				Yugoslavia	52.87
6	Ivory Coast	58.32		Philippines	52.86
	Canada	57.14		Turkey	52.77
	German		31	Colombia	52.73
	Federal Republic	56.76		Sudan	52.72
	Austria	56.62		Chile	52.65
	Thailand	56.59		Brazil	52.59
				Mexico	52.52
11	Iran	56.28			
	Lebanon	55.66	36	Indonesia	52.48
	Egypt	55.47		India	52.48
	Luxemburg	55.46		Belgium	52.38
	Netherlands	55.40		Saudi Arabia	52.13
				United States	52.12
16	Liberia	55.36			
	Japan	55.16	41	Britain	51.88
	Australia	55.14		Jordan	51.64
	New Zealand	55.00		Sierra Leone	51.54
	Finland	54.76		Burma	51.42
				Venezuela	51.37
21	Pakistan	54.57			
	Ireland	53.90	46	Ethiopia	51.04
	Morocco	53.68		Tunisia	50.92

TABLE 1 – *Continued*

Rank	Nation	Score	Rank	Nation	Score
	Taiwan	50.83	81	Bulgaria	46.94
	Togo	50.77		Malagasy Republic	46.92
	Portugal	50.60		Ecuador	46.92
				Tanzania	46.88
51	Hungary	50.39		Mauretania	46.80
	Ghana	50.36			
	Spain	50.14	86	Libya	46.76
	Peru	50.09		Upper Volta	46.54
	France	49.95		Dominican Republic	46.40
				Cambodia	46.39
56	Israel	49.92		Panama	46.09
	Zaire	49.78			
	South Korea	49.70	91	Niger	45.94
	Senegal	49.69		Syria	45.89
	Afghanistan	49.62		Honduras	45.75
				Paraguay	45.68
61	Mali	49.56		Costa Rica	45.52
	Romania	49.42			
	Nigeria	49.41	96	Uruguay	45.50
	Sri Lanka	49.32		Haiti	44.91
	South Vietnam	49.16		Cyprus	44.40
				Zambia	44.06
66	Algeria	48.78		Congo	43.86
	Czechoslovakia	48.59			
	Malaysia	48.35	101	South Africa	43.65
	Cameroon	48.28		Dahomey	43.37
	Nicaragua	48.25		Somalia	43.34
				Chad	42.88
71	Guinea	47.99		Gabon	42.53
	U.S.S.R.	47.86			
	Cuba	47.79	106	Kenya	42.00
	Guatemala	47.67		Jamaica	41.94
	Poland	47.51		Yeman Republic	41.60
				Uganda	40.96
76	Bolivia	47.51		El Salvador	40.03
	Central				
	African Republic	47.42	111	Albania	39.78
	Argentina	47.28		Mongolia	39.18
	Nepal	47.10		Malawi	38.79
	Laos	47.03		Malta	35.03

SOURCE: Tables 1, 2, and 3 are drawn from "National Support for World Order: A Research Report" by Robert C. Angell and are reprinted from *Journal of Conflict Resolution* Vol. 17, No. 3 (September 1973) pp. 429–54 by permission of the Publisher, Sage Publications, Inc.

Table 1 is subject to misinterpretations of two kinds. On the one hand, the differences between nations scoring close together should be given little weight. Since we cannot be sure that a given measure of support for world order has the same validity in every country, we cannot assume that the rank order of nations is accurate. On the other hand, one should not conclude that the table tells little. Using seven indicators as the basis of the NSWO index yields a much higher probability that a superior score represents superiority-in-fact, than would using a single indicator. Perhaps one can say, with some confidence, that a nation two full points (2.00) above another is showing greater support for world order.

This standard of interpretation permits, in general, only very broad statements about the placement of nations: the economically developed nations tend to be in the upper half of the list and the developing nations in the lower half; the Western European nations tend to be higher than the members of the Communist bloc. At the very top of the list, however, we can be more specific. Switzerland is clearly the single outstanding country in support for world order and the trio of Denmark, Sweden, and Norway clearly form a Scandinavian group that deserves to be rated next. These results have surprised no one who is in touch with world affairs. Switzerland has long had a policy of positive neutrality—not to become involved in the wars fought by its powerful neighbors, but to lend active support to efforts to achieve permanent peace. Its leadership in the foundation of the International Red Cross is but one example. Switzerland's selection as the site of the headquarters of the League of Nations and its willingness to play host to the International Labour Organization and the World Health Organization are others.

The three Scandinavian nations also have a worldwide reputation for nonbelligerence and positive efforts to attain world peace. Sweden has followed a policy of neutrality ever since the Napoleonic wars; Norway and Denmark (though they joined the North Atlantic Treaty Organization after suffering invasion by Germany during World War II) are, like Sweden, members of the Nordic Union, an organization committed to a policy of international peace.

The position of Switzerland, Denmark, Sweden, and Norway at the top of the list not only confirms what has been the perception of international relations scholars for thirty years, but, reciprocally, lends validity to the NSWO index.

My research on national support for world order was begun in the late 1960s with data centering on 1966. The NSWO index aimed to express efforts and activities that foster a system of relations among nations capable of creating and maintaining world peace. I had in mind such particular goals as cooperation among nations, an effective web of international organizations, and widespread commitment to the cause of peace. Certainly the horrors of war were in the forefront of attention.

Well into this century, peace had been seen almost entirely as avoidance of conflict over territorial claims; nations saw the world as divided into sovereign territories—territories which their possessors used for the satisfaction of their interests, whether in national resources, living space, standard of living, practice of a particular religion, or pursuit of an ideology. Those interests could be satisfied on national territories and the people of each nation wanted as much of their satisfaction as they could get at a tolerable cost. Peace was thus a balance struck through the competitive exercise of power.

Peace, increasingly since 1919, has come to emphasize less the separateness of states and to give more attention to common problems that call for common solutions. In other words, world order requires more than a structure of negotiation and arbitration. It requires a structure that can create and administer rules for situations hitherto not subject to rules. The Index of National Support for World Order, with its seven components, is only partly responsive to this need. When the United Nations was founded more than thirty years ago, peace and security were the watchwords.

How many then saw that nations would have to worry about the pollution of their common atmosphere and their common oceans? How many then realized that shortages in energy and mineral resources would soon become bones of contention requiring world attention? How many foresaw a threat of world overpopulation that would bring the charge of irresponsibility to nations that did nothing about high rates of natural increase? These are problems on which world attention is now focused, and national support for world order today implies serious attempts to cope with them. To be complete, the NSWO index should be measuring national efforts to contribute solutions to these problems, but as yet there has been no systematic marshalling of comparative data on such efforts. Thus, the NSWO index is already dated.

So far the study had determined a rough order among 114 nations in their support for world order. The next task was to discover why they had fallen in that order. This required find a small set of national characteristics that could qualify as causal influences because they could do well in predicting the scores on the NSWO index if those scores were not known. Since positions on the scale of support for world order presumably result from governmental policies, these causal influences (hereafter called predictors) might be any characteristics that were likely to affect those policies. The search for these predictors was guided by social science theory. For technical reasons, it would have been desirable to use predictors that were independent of each other (not closely correlated), but unfortunately this desirable goal was not achieved.

A former study of mine had indicated that several kinds of transnational participation probably had significant effects on attitudes toward other cultures and peoples.[8] The kind easiest to measure for most countries was citizen participation in international nongovernmental organizations (INGOs). Each edition of the *Yearbook of International Organizations* lists, for each organization, the countries from which its membership is drawn. These memberships usually represent groups, like the

American Political Science Association in the International Political Science Association. Sometimes the members are individual citizens. Using the 1966–67 edition of the *Yearbook*, I counted the INGOs of worldwide rather than regional scope in which each country was represented within the following sections: bibliography, press; social sciences; international relations; agriculture; transport, travel; technology; science; education, youth; health, medicine; arts, literature, radio; and sport, recreation. I ignored listings in eight other sections because it seemed to me that organizations to be found in them were not equally relevant to the life of all countries and that their inclusion might, therefore, bias the results. There were 523 appropriate INGOs listed in the sections covered. The number of INGO memberships ranged from 495 for France to 0 for Yemen. This predictor is called INGO participation.

In *Nationalism and Social Communication*, Karl W. Deutsch argued that elementary education, reading newspapers, and listening to radio broadcasts prepared citizens for effective participation in national affairs.[9] It seemed likely that the same experiences would prepare the people of a nation for world affairs. If one made the further assumption that effective participation would generate support for world order, one had a promising hypothesis. I therefore constructed a second predictor, labeled enlightenment, which combined measures for school enrollment, newspaper circulation, and radio listening.

Obviously, nations that have a great need for trade will favor world order, but how does one determine which countries have a great need for trade? I used a suggestion of the Norwegian scholar, Johan Galtung, who theorized that trade was most urgent for a small country with a high gross national product per capita. Such a nation cannot maintain its standard of living without mass production of specialized products, and this requires heavy exports. Conversely, a large country with a low national GNP per capita has less need of foreign trade because it has a low degree of specialization and a large domestic market. I operationalized this idea by using the ratio of GNP per capita divided by the population. I added a secondary component, actual foreign trade for each country, since the desire to attain a stable world order is affected not merely by the need for trade but by the habit of it. I called the predictor urgency of foreign trade.

The fourth predictor, population pressure, is a negative force. The hypothesis is that the more severe the population pressure, the fewer are the resources, human and material, to support anything so remote as world order. Population pressure, however, was considered to be more than just a matter of rate of growth. It was assumed that pressure was less or greater according to the country's economic capability for coping with that growth. Thus the greatest pressures were recorded for poor countries with high rates of natural increase.

The final predictor was called productivity in relation to reference nations. The theory of relative deprivation in social psychology—that what is important is not the absolute amount of deprivation but the amount relative to that of natural rivals—was its source. Economic success relative to other countries felt to be "in the same league" was hypothesized to give a nation a sense of high status that would express itself in efforts to realize a more orderly world. The reference groups in which standings were determined for each nation were the following five: the Latin American countries; the developed Western countries (including those in Europe and North America, with the addition of South Africa, Turkey, Japan, Australia and New Zealand); the Communist Eurasian countries; the sub-Saharan African countries (except South Africa); and, finally, other Asian countries and North African countries.

At least twelve other predictors were rejected as unsuitable. Either data on them were not available for enough countries, or they were so closely related to one of the five chosen as to provide no added leverage, or, after trial, they were discovered to have weak correlations with the NSWO index.

Table 2 shows the relation of the five predictors with the

seven indicators of support for world order. Since correlations less that 0.20 are inconsequential, only twenty of the forty are at all significant. It is clear from inspection that INGO participation is, generally speaking, the most powerful predictor. Enlightenment is next. Population pressure, a negative influence, was expected to have negative coefficients, but turned out to be the least powerful. The predictors collectively are most successful in predicting contributions/assessments, cooperation/conflict, and IGO memberships. They are least successful in predicting Red Cross contributions. These relations are shown graphically in figure 1, which charts only correlations of more than 0.20 with the separate indicators (light lines) and the NSWO index (heavy lines). There is only one light line from population pressure because the remainder of its correlations were less than 0.20.

The single highest correlation in table 2, that between INGO participation and IGO membership, is easily under-

TABLE 2

Correlations of the Predictors with the Seven
Separate Indicators and with the NSWO Index

	Contributions/ Assessments	Absences and Abstentions	Diplomatic Representation	Bilateral Treaty References	Cooperation/ Conflict	Red Cross Contributions	IGO Memberships	NSWO Index
INGO participation	.39	.24	.48	.19	.42	–.00	.62	.56
Enlightenment	.44	.17	.30	.05	.33	.05	.41	.44
Urgency of foreign trade	.45	.07	–.01	.21	.18	.31	.01	.31
Population pressure	–.03	–.22	–.07	–.07	.04	–.07	–.17	–.15
Productivity relative to reference nations	.31	.30	.15	.17	.18	.22	.12	.38

NOTE: N varies between 88 and 114. For those interested in statistical significance levels, coefficients as high as .25 would be significant at the .01 level (one-tailed test).

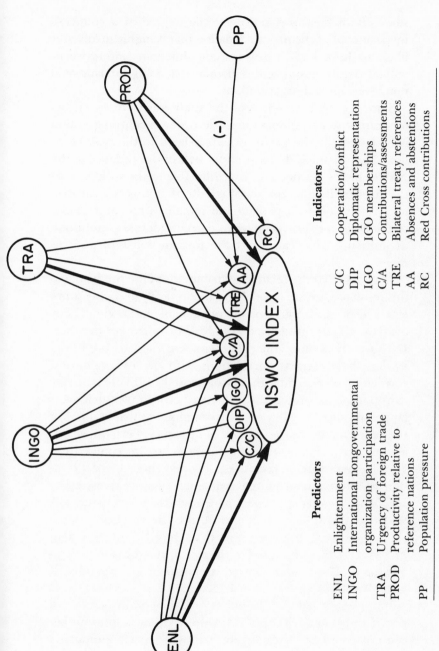

Predictors

ENL   Enlightenment
INGO   International nongovernmental
        organization participation
TRA   Urgency of foreign trade
PROD   Productivity relative to
        reference nations
PP   Population pressure

Indicators

C/C   Cooperation/conflict
DIP   Diplomatic representation
IGO   IGO memberships
C/A   Contributions/assessments
TRE   Bilateral treaty references
AA   Absences and abstentions
RC   Red Cross contributions

Fig. 1. Correlations of more than 0.20 between predictors and separate and combined indicators

stood. Both measures represent the degree of a country's international participation. A nation that is highly involved is likely to have both a government that joins intergovernmental organizations and a people that joins international nongovernmental organizations.

Since the main objective of the study was to discover factors causative of support for world order, a central question is how strongly the predictors are related to the NSWO index. The answer is that just under half of the variance in the NSWO index, 47 percent, is attributable to the influence of the five predictors. For social science data this is a satisfactory result. That 53 percent still remains with cause undetermined is not surprising when one considers the multitude of influences that can affect the foreign policy of governments.

If we ask what the relative contributions of the predictors to this result are, we are faced with a theoretically insoluble problem. The predictors are not independent of one another. They overlap in their influence on the NSWO index. For instance, INGO participation and enlightenment, the two predictors having the strongest correlations with the index, have a correlation coefficient with each other of 0.76. There is no way to apportion accurately the influence between two such overlapped predictors. They each make unique contributions, but they also create a shared stream of influence. Perhaps we can assume, in this case, that the common stream comes from knowledge of foreign countries, obtained either by participation in international nongovernmental organizations, or by schooling, the reading of newspapers, and listening to radio. A tentative allocation of influence to the five predictors separately, however, was so necessary to the forecasting of changes in NSWO scores (discussed in chapter 5) that I made such an allocation. The method I used is explained in appendix A. The allocations appear in table 3.

It can be argued that the power of INGO participation as a predictor of national support for world order is spurious because it could be a result, not a cause, of such support. I

TABLE 3
Percentages of Influence Allocated
to Five Predictors

INGO participation	21%
Enlightenment	11%
Urgency of foreign trade	8%
Productivity relative to reference nations	6%
Population pressure	1%
Total	47%

examined this possibility by looking at the INGO participation scores of the Communist countries. It is usually assumed that they have discouraged their citizens from participating in international nongovernmental organizations (we know that they have often frowned upon attendance at foreign meetings). We should therefore expect, if the argument has any validity, that the INGO participation ranks of these countries would be no higher than their NSWO ranks. To my surprise, each of them (except Albania) had a higher rank on INGO participation than on the NSWO index. In other words, there was no evidence that governmental policy was determining the degree of participation in nongovernmental organizations.

Since INGO participation must be seen as causal, we can only conclude that in the conferences and other activities sponsored by international nongovernmental organizations, participants from different countries learn to work together and to appreciate one another's cultures. My study mentioned earlier supports this conclusion.[10] It is probable that other forms of transnational participation dealt with in that work, such as study abroad, would also have been predictive of the scores on the NSWO index if worldwide data had been available.

It is no surprise that enlightenment is predictive of support for world order, but it is, perhaps, surprising that it is not more predictive than it is. One would think that broadened horizons would make for anxiety about international conflict. Intellectuals and sophisticates are usually thought to be critical of narrow nationalism. Perhaps the reason that the relation is not stronger is that most education and much reading has a vocational, not a political purpose.

The finding that urgency of foreign trade is a significant influence toward support for world order also needs little comment. Nations whose lifeblood is import and export naturally are fearful that war, even if it does not involve them directly, will interrupt the vital flow. Embargoes and blockades in wartime are a serious matter to noncombatants.

It is worth mention that trade makes countries generally dependent on others, but not necessarily dependent on *particular* others. Thus, the United States needs to import tea—but if it does not get it from China, it can get it from Indonesia or Sri Lanka. Of course, the scarcer the needed resource is, the more likely that the importers of it become dependent on particular countries.

It is interesting that the rather farfetched hypothesis of a positive connection between the economic status of a nation among its perceived peers and its support for world order proved to have some validity. There seems to be an element of noblesse oblige here: those whom the world has treated well feel obligated to support world order. This finding suggests that reference group analysis might be useful in other aspects of international relations.

Although population pressure proved to have a small negative correlation with the NSWO index, as hypothesized, it contributed only 1 percent of the causal influence. This is so trivial an amount that it may well be a chance finding. Hence I shall ignore it.

The causal influences (predictors) used in the study account for less than half of the variance in national support for world order. Other causal factors that were not identified may be of several kinds. A glance at the rank order of nations in table 1, with many developed European nations near the top, might lead to the guess that affluence would be a significant predictor. I did not choose it originally because

I had no theoretical reason to expect that gross national product per capita would be an important positive influence. My own research on American cities using the 1940 census had shown that level of living was not significantly correlated with the social integration of a city;[11] and the literature on international relations did not suggest that national support for world order would be positively related to affluence. Since table 1 yields a contrary possibility, I have checked the relationship and find that the correlation of GNP per capita with national support for world order is 0.492. If it had been included in table 2, its correlation with the NSWO index would have been much less than that of INGO participation but more than that of enlightenment. The conclusion, however, that it should therefore have been an original predictor does not follow, for when affluence is added to the five original predictors, that addition only increases the multiple coefficient of determination from 0.470 to 0.498. This is because affluence is largely expressing itself through the original predictors, especially enlightenment, urgency of trade, and INGO participation. It is a background factor that fosters them and they in turn foster national support for world order.

It is likely, however, that there are other proximate predictors that would have proved to be significant, such as differences among societies in their internal class relations. Unfortunately the research has not been done that would make it possible to test this hypothesis. Surprisingly, I found that variations in political systems from absolute monarchy to full democracy had little independent influence once the effect of enlightenment had been taken into account. Undoubtedly, differences in the effectiveness of national leaders would be a significant causal influence, but no one has yet found a valid measure for this variable.

In order to be sure that the study under discussion had not become irrelevant to the world of 1975, I obtained the data for 1969–74 on contributions/assessments, which was the most representative component of the original NSWO index. The scores of the countries this time had a correlation of 89.2 with their earlier scores. Since the midpoints of the two time series were seven years apart, stability in contributions/assessments, and, less certainly, in the NSWO index as a whole seems evident. There are noticeably greater shifts in scores among the developing, than among the developed, countries. This is not surprising when one considers that many of them became nations only in the sixties. Their first decade was a period of adaptation.

The data on support for world order reveal that nations have quite different priorities in allocating their national efforts and resources. Some are much more concerned with global tasks and problems than others. The data on predictors help to explain why this is so. These explanations will be useful in discussing the actual and potential contributions of particular nations to world order in subsequent chapters.

Table 1 has already made one point clear. Highly homogeneous nations are not necessarily narrowly nationalistic. Norway is the perfect exemplar—almost all of her population is of Norwegian nationality and yet she is a leader in support of world order. But at the same time, Norwegians are deeply patriotic. This combination of national traits gives a foretaste of what will be much discussed later. Some nations seem to be forsaking, or at least modifying, traditional nationalism.

4
The Pioneers

The research reported in the last chapter showed four countries to be outstanding in national support for world order—Switzerland, Denmark, Sweden, and Norway. They achieved that distinction by virtue of their scores on seven appropriate indicators. Since they seem to be leaders in a direction less nationalistic than most other nations, it is proper to dub them pioneers. Before going further, however, it will be prudent to see whether this status is confirmed by evidence not used in assigning them top ratings.

The uniqueness of the Swiss national development has been long in the making. Composed of a group of small cantons whose federation begin in 1291, what is now Switzerland has always been surrounded by more powerful neighbors—during the last 100 years by France, German, Austria, and Italy. From the end of the Thirty Years' War in 1648, that great religious struggle pitting Catholics against Protestants, these powerful neighbors have competed for preeminence in Central Europe. For three centuries wars between Austrians and Italians, French and Italians, French and Germans, and Austrians and Germans, including the two world wars, swirled around the Swiss borders. These struggles always threatened to boil over into Swiss territory as each side sought to gain advantage.

Under these circumstances it is no wonder that the Swiss adopted a policy of neutrality. As early as 1515 they received a bitter lesson. During an expansionary foray into Italy they were severely defeated by French forces in league with Venice. A century later, when the Thirty Years' War broke out, the cantons (half Catholic, half Protestant) realized that the federation would be torn apart if they became involved. They wisely declared their neutrality, making a virtue of necessity. The Treaty of Westphalia in 1648 recognized the neutral status of the Swiss Confederation. Thereupon, the confederation adopted a strong defense policy and forebade the passage of foreign troops through its territory.

Another and quite different aspect of Swiss development was influential in shaping the distinctive character of the country. This was the cooperative struggle of the cantons to rid themselves of the supervising authority of the Holy Roman Empire (a struggle made famous by Schiller's *William Tell*). Each canton prided itself on its autonomy, but they had to work closely together if they were to win their joint independence. Since there were periodic disagreements among the eight members of the confederation at that time, they hit upon the novel practice of asking a nonmember canton— Appenzell —to mediate disputes between them. Later, when the confederation expanded to thirteen cantons, three of them were declared special mediators for the whole system. These three did not have to wait for an invitation to mediate, but were authorized to step in whenever a dispute became serious. One scholar suggests that the unity of Switzerland today comes not from nationalism, but from centuries of experience during which the cantons have negotiated with one another.[1]

After 1648, the Swiss Confederation saw itself, and was seen by others, as a peacemaker among the great states of Europe. It was given this role on a number of occasions. Once, at least, the confederation tried to mediate a civil war (between Charles I of England and Cromwell) but was unsuccessful in its attempt.

Switzerland's peculiar role was not always recognized, however. Louis XIV of France forced the confederation into an alliance which violated its neutrality, and at the end of the eighteenth century Switzerland was invaded by Napoleon's army. In the Treaty of Paris (1814), after the final downfall of Napoleon at Waterloo, Switzerland was given a guarantee of perpetual neutrality and of the inviolability of her territory. The Swiss were still not strong enough, however, to exert much influence in European politics. Austria, for instance, forced the confederation to renounce for a decade its traditional practice of giving asylum to political refugees. Because of this weakness, Switzerland changed its legal character in 1848 from a confederation to a federal state, thus following in the path blazed by the United States sixty years earlier. This strengthened the hand of the central government in dealing with the surrounding powers. When the Gotthard tunnel under the Alps was opened in 1882, these powers decided to continue the guarantee of Swiss independence. They judged Switzerland strong enough to resist invasions aiming to close the tunnel.

Consistent with their long established humanitarian bent, the Swiss set up in 1864 the International Committee of the Red Cross, with headquarters in Geneva. The first worldwide intergovernmental organization, the Universal Postal Union, was established in Berne in 1875. Since then Switzerland, perhaps because of its centuries of neutrality has been regarded as natural seat for international institutions: among them, the now defunct League of Nations, the International Telecommunications Union, the International Labour Organization, the World Health Organization, and the World Meterological Organization. Including both intergovernmental organizations and international nongovernmental organizations, 325 bodies have their headquarters in Switzerland—11.3 percent of the world total of 2,877 in 1974. Only France, Belgium, the United Kingdom, and the United States are hosts to more. International headquarters such as these undoubtedly are both effect of Swiss receptivity and cause of Swiss cosmopolitanism.

Another influence that is probably at work in all small,

well-educated countries is the tendency for their writers, artists, and scientists to expand their horizons by temporary residence abroad. Combined with the lack of a strong national culture in the Swiss case, the result is intellectuals who are broadly European in their outlook. It is an easy step from there to a world perspective.

World Wars I and II found the Swiss following their ancient policy of neutrality. At the founding of the League of Nations, they were given a special exception to the constitutional obligation to participate in collective action against an aggressor. They have not joined the United Nations because of its similar requirement, but they have joined all of the U.N. Specialized Agencies that conduct humanitarian programs throughout the world.

At the present writing, the Swiss are involved in four expanding circles of international activity. (1) With their neighbors, they are currently attempting to develop treaties to deal with the cross-border problems in the metropolitan areas of Geneva and Basel. (2) In Western Europe, Switzerland is a member of the Council of Europe and the European Free Trade Association; it has also signed a free-trade treaty (for most items) with the European Economic Community. (3) In Europe as a whole, the Swiss favor more Pan-European cooperation and are therefore cultivating trade and cultural relations with the eastern European countries. (4) In the world, the Swiss have been getting more involved in aid to developing countries—humanitarian aid, not aid for political purposes. They are modernizing the administration of the Red Cross and continue to engage in other good works, such as a mission to repatriate persons displaced during the war of secession of Bangladesh from Pakistan, and the granting of asylum to political refugees from Chile after the 1973 coup there. Switzerland has also offered to Israel and the Arab states its territory as a place to negotiate.

Because of the Swiss policy of neutrality and its refusal to assume any regional or universal obligations of mutual security, some students of international affairs have labeled her isolationist. This appears to be an inapt characterization. Switzerland is independent in terms of intergovernmental political structure but is very much involved in the U.N. specialized agencies, international nongovernmental organizations, and humanitarian activities.

That the people of Switzerland, in general, favor the foreign policy that their government pursues is shown by a 1972 public opinion poll. More than 68 percent described themselves as satisfied with the government and 65 percent as having confidence in their government all or most of the time. The same proportion believed the Swiss political system to be either very good or good enough.

Two students of Switzerland have recently summed up Swiss foreign policy as having four goals: the right to trade with any nation, to grant political asylum, to act as intermediary between belligerents, and to provide humanitarian service to those in need.[2] In 1946 a great Swiss historian wrote words that still seem to ring true:

> To be truly Swiss does not exclude the sense of humanity as a whole, but fosters it or even requires it, for the crampedness of the Confederation demands as a compensation some super-national breadth. To be Swiss only is to be un-Swiss. But it is only as a sovereign state that Switzerland can fulfill her tasks of humane neutrality. Thus the utilitarian instrument of neutrality may serve for the realization of ethical aims.[3]

It is interesting to speculate whether (in addition to the influence of Switzerland's history, its high level of enlightenment, the participation of its citizens in international nongovernmental organizations, and the urgency of its foreign trade) the high standing in support for world order is a product of the Swiss political structure. The independence of the cantons for six centuries in the confederation and their quasi autonomy for 130 years in the federation, together with their membership in four linguistic communities (German, French, Italian, and Romansch), have given the Swiss a pluralistic experience almost unique among nations. Such experience may have made them more aware of the need to put oneself in the shoes of the other, thus learning not only tolerance but cooperation and trust. Moreover, they have had much practice in negotiation among the cantons and have proven that peoples of different languages and cultural backgrounds can live together both peacefully and effectively.

Since three Scandinavian nations follow directly after Switzerland in support for world order, and since the three— Sweden, Norway, and Denmark—have had close ties and similar cultures since the beginning of the fourteenth century (though occasionally at war with one another), their histories are intertwined. Unlike Switzerland, they were governed by absolute monarchs until after the Napoleonic Wars. Their histories to that point, and even beyond, do not forecast their contemporary position as pioneers in support for world order. They were less developed than the European countries to the south and were plagued by struggles between their kings and their constitutionally weak parliaments. Sweden became part of the coalition against Napoleon and lost territory south of the Baltic that it never recovered. Denmark, which alienated England by its refusal to join in the fight against Napoleon, suffered great economic hardship. In addition, during the nineteenth century, it struggled with Germany over the possession of Schleswig-Holstein, a struggle that was lost. Norway, which had been subject to Denmark for four centuries, managed to remain neutral and unaffected by the Napolenonic Wars. But at their end, Norway was awarded to Sweden in recompense for its lost territory. Norway refused to become subject to Sweden, but in 1814 it did enter a union with Sweden. Norway did not become an independent state until 1905. Sweden and Norway took a neutral stance in all the struggles of the nineteenth century. During the course of that century, the kings of the three countries lost most of their prerogatives and became constitutional monarchs in the British mold.

At the outbreak of World War I, all three countries declared their neutrality and managed with difficulty to preserve it. Norwegian shipping prospered, but Denmark and Sweden, hemmed in by the German submarine warfare against Britain, suffered economically. This suffering, despite the success of their neutrality policy, made them welcome the creation of the League of Nations and they, together with Norway, became enthusiastic members. When Hitler took over Austria in 1937, the Sudetenland in 1938, and attacked Poland in 1939, launching World War II, the Scandinavians again declared their neutrality. Norway and Denmark, however, were drawn into the conflict in 1940 by German surprise attacks and the forcible occupation of their territories. The British navy came to the aid of the Norwegians but, when it was forced to withdraw, the Norwegian king and government also withdrew to set up a government in exile in London. Sweden maintained a shaky neutrality throughout the war and gave much aid to Danish and Norwegian refugees.

At the close of World War II, the three nations agreed that they should participate actively in the newly formed United Nations (of which Trygvie Lie of Norway was made the first secretary-general) and that they should consult closely with each other on foreign policy. Sweden favored a policy of armed neutrality for itself and a Nordic defense community for the three. Norway and Denmark, because of their unhappy experience in World War II, believed that a Nordic defense community would be too weak and, furthermore, that it would be dominated by Sweden. Between 1945 and 1948, Norway was well disposed toward the Soviet Union and adopted a policy of bridge-building between the Great Powers. In practice, this was little different from Sweden's policy of neutrality. The Communist coup in Czechoslovakia in 1948 shocked all three countires; Norway and Denmark joined the North Atlantic Treaty Organization in 1949, stipulating that no foreign troops should be stationed on their territories. For three reasons, Sweden refused to join NATO: from fear of Soviet reaction, because of its neutrality policy, out of sympathy for Finland's precarious position on the Soviet border. Sweden has shown its independence of the anti-Communist bloc by its U.N. voting record. It has paralleled United States policy only 50–60 percent of the time, as against 70–80 percent for Denmark and Norway.

In 1953 Sweden, Norway, and Denmark were joined by Finland and Iceland in forming the Nordic Council—an interparliamentary organization with a nationally mixed secretariat. The council meets annually with cabinet members of the five countries and other members of the parliaments in attendance. They discuss common problems that have been put on the agenda by the collective executive, composed of the five foreign ministers. A study of the Nordic Council in 1967 concluded:

> The conclusion remains that, after a dozen years of operation, the Council has not succeeded in systematic penetration of the governments, either as an external pressure group or as an integral part of government. The level of intergovernmental cooperation is high, but the executive chooses the topics and sets the pace. The governments believe that the bulk of inter-Scandinavian activity must remain in the governmental plane and that the main task of the Council is to "mold opinion," to try to engage our countrymen, to interest them, to make them enthusiastic, as far as possible over the ideas [put forward] in the Nordic Council.[4]

Even though the author minimizes the influence of the council on the policies of the several governments, it is a fact that the scores of Sweden, Norway, and Denmark are remarkably similar on the four indicators of support for world order that are related to the United Nations. A student of contemporary Scandinavia comments on this similarity of view as follows: "The Nordic countries provide a case study in successful cooperation salvaged from thwarted integration. . . . The five swans of the North fly together in remarkable harmony."[5] This general policy is expressed in many different activities of the individual Scandinavian states.

Sweden is the largest of the three, both in size and population, and the wealthiest in GNP per capita. It has become renowned throughout the world as having an economy half capitalist and half socialist, exemplifying "the middle way."[6]

Sweden, unlike Norway and Denmark, refused to join NATO. It has preferred a policy of nonalignment, peaceful coexistence, and mediation. Unlike Switzerland, Sweden joined the United Nations and agreed to support its actions if they were consonant with the charter. The invasion of South Korea by North Korea (with the backing of the Soviet Union and China in 1950) and the ensuing resolution in the Security Council calling for collective action against the aggressor posed a problem for Sweden's active neutrality. Sweden had not expected that the United Nations would be able to act in a conflict involving the Great Powers and did not want to be in the position of exacerbating such a conflict. The nation compromised by sending a hospital to the war zone, but no troops. On the other hand, the Swedish people were so outraged by the Soviet intervention in Hungary in 1956 that they voted for the U.N. resolution of protest. Similarly, they strongly protested the Soviet invasion of Czechoslovakia in 1968. Sweden has responded to U.N. calls for peacekeeping personnel more often than any other nation—ten times. The biggest operations were those in the Middle East, Zaire, and Cyprus. Like Norway, Denmark, and Finland, Sweden has earmarked forces that are ready on a standby basis for U.N. peacekeeping. The four contingents have been jointly trained. The second secretary-general of the United Nations, the Swede Dag Hammarskjold, died in an airplane crash while visiting the peacekeeping operation in Zaire.

Sweden's greatest interest in the United Nations has been to achieve disarmament. It was a leader in the Eighteen-Nation Disarmament Committee which sponsored both the banning of nuclear testing in the air, the waters, and space, and the agreement for the nonproliferation of nuclear weapons. Ms. Alva Myrdal of Sweden was a member of the Committee from 1962 to 1973. The Stockholm International Peace Research Institute (a nongovernmental organization) has been making valuable scientific studies since 1968.

The Swedish government took the lead in getting the United Nations to hold the International Conference on the Environment which, after several years of work under a British secretary-general, was held in Stockholm during the summer of 1972. This conference laid out programs of research and action of great potential significance.

Sweden has joined the Council of Europe, whose members are drawn from national parliaments, but has refused to join the European Economic Community, presumably because most of its members belong to NATO. (The Soviet Union, a neighbor across the Baltic, might take offense.) Sweden is, however, a member of the European Free Trade Association. It was one of nine U.N. members that in 1965 introduced a resolution calling for greater cooperation among countries of Eastern and Western Europe. It has increased its trade with the Soviet Union and the other Communist states. Aid to underdeveloped countries is one of the prime interests of all the Scandinavian nations. Like the others, Sweden has adopted the policy of giving no aid with a view to political benefits. All its funds are devoted to humanitarian help. Sweden has never had colonies and is very careful not to lay itself open to the charge of neocolonialism. About a third of its aid is given to the programs of the United Nations supported by nations collectively. Two-thirds goes directly to under-developed countries, partly because Sweden wishes to support programs aimed to slow population growth, which are not sponsored by the United Nations.

That there is strong mass support for foreign aid in Sweden is shown by a Gallup poll of 1968: 38 percent of those questioned believed that help should be given, even if it meant that Sweden's own economic progress would be retarded; another 41 percent believed that foreign aid should be given as long as

it did not slow national progress. Sweden is one of three nations that has exceeded the percentage of annual GNP (0.7 of
1%) set as a goal by the United Nations for contributions by
developed countries to developing countries. In general, the
masses in Sweden seem to feel that they are well represented by
their leaders and hence trust them to make wise decisions.
This, in turn, allows the leaders to adopt rational, farseeing
policies without having to worry about shortsighted citizen
pressures. A foreign minister of Sweden has written:

> For a small country like Sweden . . . the existence of
> solid popular support for its foreign policy is a source of
> strength. The country is thereby enabled to pursue a firm
> and consistent course; this in turn helps us retain the
> confidence of the world outside. Other countries do not
> have to doubt or speculate about the main objective of
> our foreign policy. They should be able to know where
> we stand and to count on our adherence to the policy we
> have chosen. It has been our constant endeavor to build
> up such a capital of foreign trust in us. This capital is a
> valuable asset. And it is my conviction—based on the
> testimony of leading statesmen—that we have achieved
> this aim, that we have come into possession of a capital of
> trust.[7]

A Norwegian student of international affairs has characterized Sweden's foreign policy as no less globally humanitarian
than those of Denmark and Norway but perhaps less warm,
more rational, and calculating. This would be compatible with
the greater size and complexity of Swedish society and the
consequent greater impersonality of its internal relations. If
still larger nations become as supportive of world order as
these three Scandinavian nations, they will probably do so
more in the style of Sweden than of Norway and Denmark.

Norway is the least populous of the four pioneer nations. It
is geographically the most peripheral and was the last to indus-
trialize. It is one of the most homogeneous nations in the

world, having no significant minority. Like its neighbors, Sweden and Denmark, it embraces a moderate socialism. It has long had economic ties with Great Britain; and the British attempt to stem the sweep of the Nazi invasion of Norway in 1940 and to receive the government-in-exile created sentimental ties, as well. Norway has been described as the "most Atlantic" of the Nordic nations. When the Cold War started in 1948, Norway, having rejected a Nordic defense union as too weak, joined NATO as a security measure. It has tried hard, however, to be friendly with the Soviet Union and to increase its trade with her giant neighbor.

Shipbuilding and shipping have been the most lucrative of Norway's industries. Despite its tiny population, Norway's commercial fleet is the third largest in the world. Peaceful transport by sea is therefore essential to the nation's prosperity (5 percent of its GNP derives from shipping charges). During the last decade a new source of income of great promise has been discovered—rich oil fields under the North Sea. Norway enthusiastically joined the United Nations as the best hope for the maintenance of peace and has become a member of all the specialized agencies. It began a program of foreign aid by helping the commercial fisheries of India in 1952 and since then has extended bilateral aid, through the Norwegian Agency for Development, to a number of countries. As with Sweden, the program is purely humanitarian and not designed to return political advantage. Norway gives about twice as much through the U.N. multilateral programs as through its own bilateral program. It was the first nation to follow the United States in the creation of a peace corps.

Another facet of Norwegian policy is participation in peacekeeping. It has answered the U.N. call seven times and has had military contingents in the three most difficult operations—in the Middle East, Zaire, and Cyprus. It has also been ardently supportive of disarmament and has favored a demilitarized zone in central Europe.

Norway has few ties with the Communist satellites in Eastern

Europe except Poland, with which there are long-standing mutual cultural interests. It has tried to reduce the barriers that hamper trade with these eastern countries. Norway's outspoken criticism of the 1968 armed intervention in Czechoslovakia, however, has dimmed hopes for the early realization of this ambition.

Norways' position as a small country accepted by the giants of NATO has influenced its character as a nation. A peripheral unit in a powerful organization, the nation has, in a sense, already overachieved. Its desire to keep that high status leads it to be generally content with the status quo and to work for world change slowly and cooperatively through the approved channels of the United Nations. Norway believes that interbloc relations can be improved first culturally, then economically, and last politically. In consolidating its foreign policy, Norway has been greatly helped by the absence of serious internal conflict. The nation's homogeneity and the common suffering of its people in World War II have produced a solidarity that rises superior to differences of opinion on particular issues.

Opinion and attitude on foreign policy have been studied more thoroughly in Norway than in Sweden and Denmark largely because of the University of Oslo's Institute of Social Research and the Peace Research Institute in Oslo. The *Journal of Peace Research*, published by the latter, has become a leading world journal in its field and has aroused great interest in foreign policy research in Norway.

There have been a number of studies, great and small, that have shed light on the attitudes of Norwegian people toward problems of world order. The largest study is by Helge Hveem, *International Relations and World Images*.[8] One question he asked of eighty-eight members of the foreign policy elite (parliamentarians, high civil servants, mass media leaders, and policy chiefs of interest groups) was whether Norway should concentrate on global or regional cooperation with other nations. A similar question had been asked of elites in Britain, France, and West Germany in an American study two years earlier. Hveem's table 4.6.2 shows that the global response was chosen by 41 percent of the Norwegians as compared to 12 percent of the British, 1 percent of the French, and 5 percent of the West Germans. Respondents from the other three countries chose regional or interregional cooperation much more frequently than the Norwegians.[9]

The frequency of the global orientation response among Norwegians is shown in other studies. In a comparison of Norwegian and American students conducting a simulation exercise on diplomacy, the Norwegians much more often used multinational, as opposed to binational, agencies in formal and informal institutional contacts.[10] Another study, using poll data, found that the Norwegian population favored giving the same or more technical assistance to developing nations with remarkable consistency (58 percent to 63 percent positive) across categories representing nine degrees of political mobilization.[11] The same consistency was found when respondents were asked about their optimism on disarmament: their optimism was moderate, but it was similar in degree throughout the population.[12]

It is probably hopeful that on several issues the most politically mobilized segments of the Norwegian population—well-educated, well-to-do men with white collar jobs, living in cities in the central part of the country—held a global perspective more often than did the remainder of the population. Generally speaking, their views are likely to spread to the less mobilized segments in the course of time. For instance, acceptance of the Norwegian Peace Corps was greater among the mobilized by more than 20 percent. The author believed that the less mobilized were simply not so well informed about the purposes and the operation of the peace corps.[13] Again, the mobilized proved more favorable than the less mobilized toward assisting nations that might be economically competitive with Norway by about 25 percent. In the opinion of the author, the mobilized realized that technical assistance might restructure relations between developing and developed countries, but they had accepted it.[14] In a similar vein, Hveem's foreign policy elite and what he calls the opinion makers (teachers of history and social studies in the high school, members of committees on foreign policy in political parties, journalists on foreign desks in Oslo, editors outside of Oslo, and administrative heads of interest groups) are more concerned than the general public with helping the developing countries to lessen the inequality among nations.[15] The foreign policy elite and the opinion makers probably see this as a means of reducing tension and conflict.

One of Hveem's central findings is that the foreign policy elite are more oriented toward European problems, while the opinion makers are more oriented toward world problems. Hveem interprets this as a consequence of the responsibility of the foreign policy elite for day-to-day choices in the field of practical politics, whereas the opinion makers have greater freedom to study broad trends in the world and suggest new issues for the consideration of the foreign policy elite. For instance, while the policy elite were taken up with NATO policy and whether to join the European Economic Community, the opinion makers were already canvassing the importance of the north-south conflict between the developed and the developing nations and were concerned about world hunger and overpopulation. Opinion makers were also much more inclined to give preference on customs duties to the developing countries.[16] Hveem found that the foreign policy elite, opinion makers, and the public all have positive attitudes toward the United Nations, the opinion makers especially so. Because of the scope of their thought, opinion makers see more conflict of loyalties in the world than do the foreign policy elite, whose thought is more harmoniously concentric—national, Nordic Council, NATO, and U.N. policies all nesting within one another. As a result, there is more consensus on policy among the foreign policy elite than among the opinion makers, though both groups evidence greater consensus than the public in general.[17]

Denmark is the second in size and influence of the three Scandinavian pioneers. Its geographical position makes it

more interdependent with Britain, Germany, the Netherlands, Belgium, and France than are the other two countries.
Denmark joined NATO at the same time as Norway and was
the only one of the three to accept the invitation of the Common Market to join in 1973. Before then it was a member of the
European Free Trade Association. Its position as a bridge
between the Nordic Council and the Common Market should
strengthen the international, rather than the merely regional,
orientation of the Common Market.

Like the other Scandinavians, Denmark follows global
humanitarian policies. It is active in the United Nations and
the specialized agencies. By 1968, Denmark was giving 1 percent of its GNP to bilateral and multilateral foreign aid programs, none of which was motivated by a desire for political
advantage. No other nation has achieved this percentage. In
1972, Denmark was the largest contributor per capita to the
U.N. Development Program. During the Korean conflict it
sent a hospital ship; Denmark sent aid to Biafra during the
Nigerian civil war and to Bangladesh during its secession from
Pakistan. Denmark strongly supports disarmament and has
signed all the U.N. multilateral treaties dealing with world
problems. It has furnished contingents for U.N. peacekeeping
eight times. Like Sweden and Norway, it has earmarked contingents of its armed forces for U.N. service. Like Sweden,
Denmark is one of the nine countries from both Eastern and
Western Europe that sponsored a U.N. resolution in 1965
calling for greater European economic cooperation.

The government and the public in Denmark achieved great
solidarity in the nineteenth century. The loss of Schleswig (in
the war with Germany in 1864) gave them a common goal—to
reunite the Danish people in the future. About the same time,
Bishop Grundtvig had the vision of establishing the folk high
schools. These schools did much to enlighten the farmers of
Denmark, both technically and politically. They also have done
much to give the Danish people pride in their history and
culture. At the close of World War I, the residents of the

northern part of Schleswig voted in a plebescite to return to Denmark.

Unfortunately, there are not as many studies of Danish foreign policy as of Swedish and Norwegian. One infers, from the cooperation in the Nordic Council and from roll call votes in the United Nations, that the three countries generally pursue similar policies. There are exceptions. Sweden is more neutralist than Norway and Denmark, and Norway is less willing than Denmark to merge its economic destiny with the large West European states. On support of the United Nations, disarmament, peacekeeping, and aid to underdeveloped countries they are united. Though they became supporters of world order from an inability to match the power of the large, developed countries, they now seemingly do so from positive conviction. Their reliance on the United Nations comes more from their belief in its mediating potential than from its ability to organize collective action. As individual nations, the Scandinavian pioneers are eager to be mediators whenever they can be useful.

As a sign of their common commitment to improving the lot of humanity, one-fourth of all the experts in technical assistance sent out by the United Nations have been Scandinavians. The Nordic countries have been successful in peacekeeping operations because they are large enough to take responsibility, but small enough not to arouse fears of selfish aggression.

The Scandinavians, undoubtedly, are well trusted around the world. This is not only because of their foreign policies, but also because their domestic systems are much admired. Hans Zetterberg, a Swedish sociologist, has written:

> In looking around the world today for a land of tomorrow attention is immediately drawn to the Nordic countries (particularly to Sweden). There by a combination of circumstances which also includes a measure of isolation from world wars, relative prosperity, and high literacy in social and economic science, features of social structure

have emerged that are in the cards for other developed countries. The trends may be present in other countries, but in Scandinavia they have grown longer and have met with more favorable circumstances. The trends I have in mind are not measured in simple statistics of wealth and production. They rather represent new ways to basic cultural values, new arrangements between man and fellowman and between public and private pursuits; in short, a new social order. . . .[18]

Zetterberg sees rationalism and humanitarianism as the keys to the successful welfare states that have been established: "Competitors within each nation do not have to face the roughest consequences of their losses. A system has evolved in which one can still gain both small and big winnings but one can only make small losses."[19] The Scandinavian social, economic, and political system is probably the most widely accepted model in the world.

Trust has also been created by a succession of great leaders in humanitarian causes: Nansen, the great Norwegian arctic explorer, almost single-handedly persuaded the League of Nations to issue passports for stateless refugees after World War I and earned the undying thanks of millions as a consequence; Trygvie Lie and Dag Hammarskjold, respectively a Norwegian and a Swede, piloted the United Nations through its infancy; and Count Bernadotte of Sweden was assigned to find a peaceful settlement to the Arab-Israeli confrontation of 1953. Indeed it is as a great moral force in the world, not as great economic innovators, that the Scandinavians have won their reputation as pioneers toward a better world.

If there are great similarities among the Scandinavian pioneers toward support for world order, are there similarities between them and Switzerland? Certainly Switzerland and Sweden, with their commitment to neutrality and their active cultivation of peace, have much in common. They are also the two most technologically developed of the four. On the other hand, Switzerland's unwillingness to join the United Nations differentiates her in one important respect from the Scandinavians. But even Switzerland and Norway, whose geographical positions and economies are most contrasting, have a similarity of spirit and of foreign policy that is impressive. Though Switzerland as a federal state evolved from a group of small, religiously and linguistically differentiated units (the cantons), and each of the three Scandinavian states maintains its political independence despite cultural similarity, the four pioneer societies are all thoroughly democratic, exhibit great internal solidarity, and their peoples see the world in like and hopeful terms. Perhaps most significant of all, the governments and their peoples share a value consensus.

At the beginning of this chapter, the four nations were pronounced pioneers in support of world order on the basis of a statistical study. In this chapter, the intention has been to ascertain whether that judgment is confirmed by other evidence. I have tried to get as much information as possible about the recent foreign policy positions of the governments and peoples of the four nations. There has been no screening of evidence that would have cast doubt on their character as pioneers. In fact, Switzerland and Sweden were both found to be somewhat coldly rational in their commitment to world order, the governments taking an enlightened stance quite as much from its promise of national advantage in the long run, as from warm concern for the peoples of other lands now. There is no question, however, that the added information does tend to show that the four are behaving differently from nations in the past; they are more supportive of world order and less exclusively following their narrow national interests.

The truth is that these four nations are committed to a less violent and more humane world. There is commitment by both governments and people. Patriotism—love of fatherland—remains, but not the nationalism that ignores the needs of other peoples. The citizens are proud of their country, not only for what it has accomplished for their ancestors and themselves, or promises to accomplish for their descendants, but for its sense of responsibility for the welfare of the global human enterprise. This pride in a new kind of nation deserves a new name: enlightened patriotism.

The virtue of this term is that it broadens traditional nationalism in two respects. First, the loyalty expressed is not that of an in-group, a nationality, but of the citizens of a territory. In World War I, for example, a considerable number of United States soldiers were not yet fully assimilated into American culture, but they were patriotic. Second, enlightened patriotism expresses a breadth of concern beyond the national territory itself—a concern which enlightenment about the interdependence of nations in the modern world produces. No doubt some of the loyalty of Americans in World War I was inspired by President Wilson's announced aim of "making the world safe for democracy."

Carleton J. H. Hayes, a great authority on nationalism, supported this point of view fifty years ago. He wrote: "To urge the mitigation of nationalism and the propagation of internationalism is not to decry patriotism. For it should ever be remembered that critics of public policy, even more than blind devotees, may be inspired by the truest love of native land, by real patriotism."[20] A religious man himself, Hayes believed that the selfishness of nationalism is opposed to Christian doctrine and to the doctrine of most great religions. He felt that the union of the love of country with devotion to the cause of humanity is both desirable and possible.

Writing in 1902 about the group self or "we," Charles Horton Cooley came to the same conclusion.

We could have no patriotism unless we were aware of other nations, and the effect of a definitely organized society of nations, in whose activities we all took a generous interest, would be, not to diminish patriotism, as some have unintelligently asserted, but to raise its character, to make it more vivid, continuous, varied and sympathetic. It would be like the self-consciousness of an intelligent individual in constant and friendly intercourse with others, as contrasted with the brutal self-assertion of one who knows his fellows only as objects of suspicion and hostility.[21]

One scholar believes, however, that even with the best will in the world it will be very difficult to exorcize nationalism. Ichheiser regards *unconscious* nationalism as the bane of the modern world. People who think they believe in one world are at bottom making nationalistic assumptions about the nature of that world. In other words, cultural biases run very deep and affect a person's thinking about even so unselfish an aspiration as the attainment of world order.[22] Enlightened patriotism cannot, of course, remain an individual sentiment. It must coalesce into a community of sentiment, becoming a common value that exercises normative influence over all elements of the society. As the pioneers have shown, this occurs through the leadership of the well-educated who are the first to realize the predicament of humanity and the necessity of transcending narrow nationalism to escape it.

A highly respected American political scientist has put forward a concept that facilitates thinking about enlightened patriotism. In discussing the goals of foreign policy, Arnold Wolfers coined the term "milieu goals" to denote possible features of the international context that a nation could identify and seek to realize.[23] If many nations were to achieve enlightened patriotism, they could strive together for such milieu goals as disarmament, tolerance in relations with one another, promotion of the welfare of mankind, and world law.

Enlightened patriotism is not so radical an idea as it may seem. In other relations, the acceptance of a larger responsibility as an aspect of a smaller one is frequent. A good father does not strive for his own success alone, but for the success of his family, which he has incorporated in his very self. The feeling of "we" is inseparable from "I." Similarly, families that were well-rooted in the traditional small town had pride in it and exerted themselves to foster its welfare. Loyalty to town was a natural extension of loyalty to family.

What another political scientist, Klaus Knorr, calls transnational loyalty goes even further than enlightened patriotism.

Individuals with a transnational loyalty or ideology have
a loyalty or ideology that *transcends* national loyalty or
ideology. Their loyalty and ideology surpasses loyalty
and ideological commitment to the nation-state as an
institution. Their loyalty may be to mankind, and their
ideological commitment to regional organizations or to
global supranational institutions which do not now exist
except in a rudimentary and fragmentary form, but
which they aspire to. To these individuals the territorial
nation-state has critical flaws or defects, or is doomed,
and national governments are not adequate as "the most
important mediating agency between individuals at
home and abroad." Such persons harbor a conception of
the self which is closely related to the external environment of their nation. Unlike chauvinists or isolationists,
they see transnational intercourse as a source of enrich-
ment rather than containment. They acquire a sense of
responsibility for what happens politically in other states
and for what their own government may do abroad.
They identify with fellow human beings as a group or on
a global or regional basis.[24]

Enlightened patriotism is a sentiment halfway between
traditional nationalism and loyalty to a world state. It would
assure more emphasis on the interests of humanity than would
nationalism, with less regimentation than would be exercised
by a world state. The doubt about it is whether it could become
the prevailing sentiment in enough states to be effective. Can
each nation develop a collective conscience that will discipline
its actions so as not to jeopardize the welfare of humanity? To
reach a positive conclusion, we do not have to suppose that all
citizens will be motivated by enlightened patriotism. But it
would be necessary for the policy makers to be so motivated,
since national policies are what will count.
If the territorial tie is less conducive than nationalism to

hostility toward other nations, we should expect that states without a dominant nationality would be more open to enlightened patriotism than nation-states. They would, as it were, have been practicing international relations already within their own borders. Although this is a logical expectation, it may not prove true in practice. To take some responsibility for the welfare of the world is a dangerous thought to nations accustomed to acting exclusively out of self-interest. Perhaps that thought can be entertained more easily by nations that feel confident and strong because they are of a single nationality.

In the course of this chapter, I have coined a new term, enlightened patriotism, to supplement the term used in the research project—national support for world order. Are the two really the same? Not quite. National support for world order describes governmental attitude and action. Enlightened patriotism suggest a wider collective sentiment. The difference is easily seen when a paternalistic or authoritarian society is compared with a democratic one. A democratic society is likely to have levels of support for world order and of enlightened patriotism that are fairly equivalent, since a government cannot take a political position that is far different from the sentiment of most of the people. In an authoritarian society, on the other hand, the government may give support to world order because it believes that this is a policy that will attract aid for development from the United Nations. There may not be a high level of enlightened patriotism, since it is a sentiment that cannot be imposed by a government.[25] The two phenomena are thus measurably independent of one another.

Of the two characteristics, enlightened patriotism seems more crucial for the world than national support for world order. It represents the modification of a deeply held sentiment, rather than a rational change in policy, and to that degree probably expresses more commitment. It is enlightened patriotism, therefore, whose spread will be the subject of the following chapter. The discovery that the four nations highest in support for world order are motivated by a

spirit broader than traditional nationalism is the most preg-
nant finding of the research presented. It demonstrates that
the political state is not a bar to action undertaken on behalf of
humanity. Enlightened patriotism is a sentiment that can be
cultivated and may have great significance for the future. The
more that policy makers and average citizens express it in their
lives, the less acrimony and conflict will attend the solution of
problems that threaten humanity.

5
Who Will Follow the Pioneers?

Although there are many organizations that might contribute to the creation of a just and stable world order, the most promising seem at this stage to be nations motivated by enlightened patriotism. Switzerland, Sweden, Denmark, and Norway have already shown the way, and we know some of the conditions that have made them preeminent. Nothing could be more hopeful for the world than to have other nations follow in their footsteps.

Several consequences would be almost inevitable. The web of relations among nations would thicken because communication would be facilitated. Nations would get along with each other better because their peoples would be more mutually responsive. The two great world antagonisms—between the Communist and the capitalist nations, and between the developed and the developing nations—would be softened because each group would be more appreciative of the position of the opposing group. Problem solving would be fostered, since joint efforts could be launched more easily. And, finally, the United Nations would be strengthened and the opportunity created for a wider application of international law.

Such a spread of enlightened patriotism is crucial in the next decade. There are many divisive forces at work in the contemporary world, as Heilbroner has so forcefully shown. If they are not soon offset by the growth of unifying forces, political chaos will be the result.

The research results discussed in chapter 3 are pertinent to the search for nations that might soon exemplify enlightened patriotism. Those that came closest to the pioneers in support for world order are listed just below them in table 1. One might jump to the conclusion that these are the most promising candidates. Such a conclusion, however, would be premature. For one thing, it ignores the fact that, although a general formula was developed that predicted the scores on national support for world order from the causal factors quite well, the scores for particular nations often varied markedly from the predictions.[1] Thus there were nations that overachieved (did better than would be predicted) and underachieved. Although these predictions from the formula apply to the situation between 1962 and 1968, they have relevance to the present time, too. This is because the three most powerful predictors—enlightenment, INGO participation, and urgency of trade —are tapping deep running aspects of the national societies, aspects that are likely to assert their expected influence in the long run. It may have been temporary influences that caused some of the over- and underachievement. It seems appropriate, therefore, to give weight to these predicted scores in identifying the nations that are the best prospects for enlightened patriotism.

I had decided, in computing the scores of potentiality for enlightened patriotism, to weight the actual NSWO scores three times as much as the predicted scores, but one thing bothered me: that most of the overachieving nations were developing nations. It has been alleged that governments occasionally have supported world order, not out of a regard for humanity, but in the hope of receiving aid for development in return for good global citizenship. There is no obvious way, however, to tell if a nation is overachieving because of humanitarian zeal or in the hope of reward. Democratic states, because of the openness with which their public business is conducted, probably find it harder to disguise motives than authoritarian states. The only nations that are suspect, therefore, are over-achieving, developing nations that have authoritarian governments. I decided, *for these countries only*, that the over-achievement represented in the NSWO scores should be re-duced somewhat before using the scores in computing po-tentiality for enlightened patriotism. This reduction was ef-fected by applying the Cutright Index of Representation men-tioned in chapter 4.[2]

Table 4 gives the scores on potentiality for enlightened patriotism, computed as described, for the 38 nations ranking in the top third of the 114 nations. These potentiality scores are meant to be indicative of the prospects for the late seven-ties. That there is a real difference between national support for world order and potentiality for enlightened patriotism is shown by the fact that 6 nations appear in table 4 that were not

TABLE 4
Potentiality for Englightened Patriotism of Thirty-eight Nations

Rank	Nation	Score	Rank	Nation	Score
1	Switzerland	71.72	20	Lebanon	54.37
2	Sweden	64.30	21	France	53.90
3	Denmark	64.24	22	Ireland	53.73
4	Norway	62.27	23	Ivory Coast	53.31
5	Kuwait	59.40	24	Yugoslavia	53.27
6	Canada	59.17	25	Iran	53.26
7	German Federal		26	Greece	52.98
	Republic	59.05	27	Mexico	52.86
8	Luxemburg	58.57	28	Chile	52.82
9	Netherlands	57.74	29	Egypt	52.68
10	Austria	57.55	30	Turkey	52.53
11	United States	57.08	31	Brazil	52.33
12	Australia	56.44	32	Venezuela	52.16
13	Japan	56.14	33	Israel	52.13
14	New Zealand	55.90	34	Hungary	52.05
15	Finland	55.87	35	Pakistan	51.77
16	Belgium	55.81	36	Colombia	51.60
17	Britain	55.39	37	Liberia	51.18
18	Italy	55.32	38	Morocco	51.02
19	Iceland	55.30			

among the first 38 in table 1: Britain, France, Hungary, Israel, the United States, and Venezuela. Conversely, 6 nations were ranked among the first 38 in table 1 that are absent from table 4: India, Indonesia, Iraq, the Philippines, Sudan, and Thailand. All of the first group were underachievers in national support for world order, and all of the second group were overachievers. Such changes are to be expected because table 4 introduces two elements not affecting the results in table 1: the influence of the predicted scores, which tends to correct for short-run idiosyncracies that affect the actual NSWO scores, and the reduction in scores of overachieving developing nations having authoritarian governments to allow for motivations not representing enlightened patriotism.

The most striking feature of this table is the predominance of European nations near the top of the list. Among the 19 nations in the first column, there are 9 European nations in addition to the 4 pioneers —13 in all. Four other nations have their original roots in Europe—Canada, United States, Australia, and New Zealand. Only two nations—Japan and Kuwait—have no ethnic ties with Europe. This is perhaps not surprising when one reflects that Europe gave birth to the industrial revolution which brought, in its train, extensive world trade, participation in international organizations, and high levels of education and communication. It is to be expected that Europe would be the area of the world best suited to the growth of enlightened patriotism.

The second set of 19 countries shows a much greater spread of nations around the globe. There are 5 more located in Europe, 5 in Latin America, 4 in the Middle East, 2 each in North Africa and sub-Saharan Africa, and 1 in South Asia. The presence of these widely distributed nations in the second sixth of the whole list of 114 nations gives hope that enlightened patriotism, if it becomes widely realized in Europe, can spread outward.

It would be foolish to predict from these figures the likelihood of future shifts toward enlightened patriotism of particular nations. At any moment some world crisis may occur which will sharpen conflicts and thrust even the pioneers back toward traditional nationalism. Even when table 4 is supplemented by historical data on foreign policy for each nation, it would be presumptuous to make predictions. But the following histori-cal data, when compared with the statistical results, should reveal which nations are in the best position to increase their sense of world responsibility.

The appearance of fourteen of the fifteen NATO nations in table 4 offers a convenient starting point for considering the possible spread of enlightened patriotism. Two of these nations—Denmark and Norway—have already been consi-dered in chapter 4. Two of the remaining twelve rank twenty-sixth and thirtieth in potentiality and can be dismissed quickly. Greece's and Turkey's embroilment over the rights of their rival ethnic groups on Cyprus, and Greece's experience with dictatorship between 1967 and 1974, have preoccupied both of them with narrow national concerns that are adverse to the growth of enlightened patriotism.

Ten NATO nations, ranking from six to twenty-one in table 4, are left to consider. Three of them are the small Benelux countries on the European continent—Belgium, the Nether-lands, and Luxemburg. They would seem superficially to be much like the pioneers in their need for trade and their high levels of INGO participation and enlightenment. To a degree, the data on the Netherlands and Luxemburg confirm this impression. Their actual scores on the NSWO index are high (though clearly inferior to the pioneers' scores), but they are grave underachievers — especially Luxemburg, which has a gap of -12.44 between its predicted and actual NSWO scores. Luxemburg is ranked fourteenth in actual score and eighth in potential; the Netherlands is ranked fifteenth and ninth. Both counties were charter members of the League of Nations and of the United Nations. The Netherlands has supplied the United Nations with peacekeeping contingents six times and has given widespread developmental aid to Indonesia, India, . Pakistan, Tanzania, and Colombia, in addition to its support for U.N. multilateral programs. It is the third nation to have reached the goal of giving seven-tenths of 1 percent of its annual gross national product for assistance to developing countries adopted by the U.N. General Assembly. Luxemburg, a nation of fewer than four hundred thousand people, has not been able to spread its good works so widely. Both countries have the potentiality to become future exponents of enlightened patriotism, but they have not yet shown the concern for all peoples—especially the Eastern European nations—that the pioneers have.

The record of Belgium is more spotty. Although its territory is the seat of more international organizations (IGOs and INGOs) than that of any other country, topping even Switzerland, and although Belgium was recognized before World War I as a neutral whose territory was to be inviolate (a guarantee which Germany breached), the nation has agreed to be host to the headquarters of NATO. This tends to give the appearance, at least, of strong support for a bloc but says nothing about enlightened patriotism. On the other hand, Belgium has sent five observer groups to monitor U.N. cease-fires and was one of nine small states that sponsored a U.N. resolution in 1965 favoring more East-West cooperation in Europe.

Belgium ranks only thirty-eighth on the NSWO index and is a gross underachiever (-13.75), resulting in a sixteenth rank on potentiality for enlightened patriotism. No doubt some of the underachievement is accounted for by Belgium's lack of internal harmony and by its need to devote resources and effort to abating the hostility between the Flemish and Walloon segments of its population. Whatever the causes, Belgium does not now appear ready to incorporate devotion to humankind in her patriotism.

Four large nations — Britain, the German Federal Republic, Italy, and France— complete the roster of NATO members in Europe. Only one of these, West Germany, has a high score on national support for world order. It ranks eighth on the NSWO index and is seventh in potentiality for enlightened patriotism. Besides the excellence of its educational system, its widespread mass media network, and its high rate of INGO participation, West Germany has had an added stimulus to contribute positively to world order. It has wanted to regain the good will of nations around the world which was lost when Hitler overran Central Europe, initiating World War II.

West Germany has attempted to moderate the Cold War by reaching agreements with the German Democratic Republic and by signing trade pacts with Communist countries to the east. As a means of bettering its world reputation, the nation has renounced the use of atomic and biological weapons. It joined the United Nations as soon as it was permitted. It had became a member of most of the specialized agencies much earlier.

It is peculiarly difficult to assess the potentiality of West Germany for enlightened patriotism because of the splitting of the former German nation into two states. There is no normal course of development in prospect. Do the two present states have to contemplate two separate courses, with doubtful implications for their former strong sense of national unity, or can they retain that sense and contemplate a day when they will be politically reunited? And how do these disparate vistas affect the possibility of enlightened patriotism in West Germany?

One might conclude that the ambiguity of the situation will, temporarily at least, strengthen the prospect of enlightened patriotism. A better ordered world would be a propitious context for reaching political settlements without fear of violence. To the degree that the German Federal Republic and the German Democratic Republic were separated out of fear of their combined potential military power, convincing evidence of West Germany's abandonment of aggrandizing policies and the demonstration of enduring concern for global accommodation would reassure other nations. Actually, West Germany has already been moving in that direction, as shown by her eighth rank on the NSWO index.

This hopeful tendency may not last, however. Suppose that West Germany finds it politically impossible, no matter how genuinely it embodies enlightened patriotism, to earn the world's confidence and achieve reunion with East Germany, or that it finds the German Democratic Republic uninterested if, and when, that becomes possible. What would be the reaction of the West Germans then? Might they not revert to the selfish nationalism of 1939?

Britain also suffers a handicap. Before 1900, Britain was the most powerful nation in the world. The pound sterling was the standard of international finance and British ships carried the largest share of the world's cargoes. The sun never set on its empire. Cecil Rhodes dreamt that Britain would become so preeminent that it could dominate the globe and bring the blessings of British political institutions to all peoples. History has brought an end to that dream. Britain still has a few scattered colonies, but its powerful former dominions have either left the British Commonwealth or become autonomous member nations of it, with only ties of sentiment to Britain. In reality, Britain is now a nation of sixty million people in severely straitened circumstances. The toll of two world wars in this century was heavy in both wealth and trained manpower. An elite that once controlled the destinies of a fifth of the world's population now controls a fiftieth; an economy that could formerly support a large leisure class is now scarcely viable. Retrenchment comes hard and austerity is resented.

Britain is a permanent member of the U.N. Security Council, was heavily involved in the creation of both the League of Nations and the United Nations, and has contributed directors-general to several of the specialized agencies. In other words, it has long been convinced that there must be a stronger world order. Britain has a potential score for enlightened patriotism that places it in the seventeenth position. The nation stands only forty-first on the NSWO index, not because it does not appreciate the need for peaceful trade nor because its population is unenlightened or lacking in INGO participation, but simply because its economic troubles have forced the nation to become an underachiever. Britain's actual score on the index is 14.04 points below its predicted score. Its people do not now have the good fortune that gives the Scan-

dinavians self-confidence and leads them to express the obligation they feel for the betterment of the world. Only recent oil
strikes in the North Sea might enable Britain to feel and do
likewise.

Italy is in somewhat the same position as Britain, except that
its difficulties are more political than economic. Ever since
World War II, the attempt to keep its large Communist Party
from power has resulted in coalition governments which have
successively lost the confidence of the electorate. In addition,
there have been frequent accusations of political corruption.
This lack of confidence in government has handicapped the
development of support for world order. The nation has,
however, participated in U.N. peacekeeping operations six
times. Despite the high development of northern Italy, the
underdeveloped state of southern Italy has lowered the score
on potentiality for enlightened patriotism of the whole country
to a rank of eighteen. (Southern Italy's underachievement
drags the whole nation down to an actual rank of only twenty-
four). Comparable to Britain and France in population, Italy
cannot be regarded as a small power that feels so peripheral to
NATO that it has to look to a stronger world order for security.
Under all these circumstances, it is not a promising candidate
for the spread of enlightened patriotism.

France is the last member of NATO on the European continent to be listed in table 4 (Portugal's potentiality score was too
low) and is lowest in rank. The reason France ranked fifty-fifth
in NSWO scores (table 1) seems to have been General de
Gaulle's promotion of national grandeur. He wanted France to
become a great independent force in world politics, and it was
on this ground that he refused to allow NATO headquarters to
remain on French soil. He longed for the restoration of the
French power and prestige of the eighteenth century and did
not wish France to be merely one of many nations working
together for a better world. This was reflected in the tremendous gap between predicted and actual scores on the
NSWO index (-15.78), making the nation an extreme underachiever in national support for world order. Since de Gaulle's

death that spirit of grandeur has flagged somewhat, but there are no signs of a sharp lessening of nationalistic ambition. It is France's high standing on the predictors of INGO participation and enlightenment that brings it up to the twenty-first rank in potentiality for enlightened patriotism.

The last three NATO nations under consideration are the United States, Canada, and Iceland. Though the United States rejected President Wilson's plan to join the League of Nations, it did play a central role in setting up the United Nations. During the early years, the majority of U.N. members followed American leadership. It was during this period that the American people came to think that their nation had the only right conception of world order, and that they should use their power to effect it. This is a nationalistic view that twenty-five years later seems, to most countries, incompatible with their conception of the good world. In spite of the massive aid to Europe dispensed through the Marshall Plan, and in spite of meeting assessments for the United Nations and the specialized agencies amounting then to roughly 30 percent of the total, the United States did not score well on the NSWO index, as seen in table 1. Its score was 52.12 and its rank forty. Since the U.S. is also the greatest underachiever of all (-19.85), its potential rank is much higher (eleventh). Though many American writers, clergymen, and professors have a strong sense of the nation's obligations to humanity and are faithful supporters of aid to developing countries, most citizens exhibit the traditional sort of patriotism that begrudges the foreign aid, both bilateral and multilateral, which the Unites States extends. The overwhelming fact is that the United States, with the exception of its futile and costly intervention in South Vietnam, has succeeded in maintaining its potent position in the world by a network of security organizations and treaties and that it prefers to conduct diplomacy in the traditional manner, rather than through the auspices of the United Nations. The United States has felt that its power and domestic democracy give it the right, abroad, to ignore the rights of small Latin American nations whenever that seems in the national interest. The U.S. is unlikely to accept world programs that would hamper its freedom of action, and there are few signs that enlightened patriotism will soon flourish among the American people.

Canada is a much more promising case. It has been a devoted supporter of the United Nations and the specialized agencies. Former prime minister Lester Pearson, in particular, was a leading statesman in U.N. circles. Nine times Canada has contributed troops to U.N. peacekeeping efforts, including the four biggest operations. It has given generously to the U.N. Development Program and to the new Francophone countries in Africa (presumably expressing French-Canadian sentiment). Canada has good relations with Communist countries.

Canada's rank of seven on the NSWO index shows it to be close to the pioneers, but there are circumstances that cast doubt on its soon achieving equality with them. One of the reasons Canada is a moderate underachiever is no doubt the strain caused by the dissatisfactions of the French-speaking minority. Probably more influential is its relationship with the United States. In Canada the economic ties between the two are viewed with ambivalence. It was glad to obtain American capital in the early period of Canadian industrial development and is grateful still for the employment (at high wages) that American investment produces, but the influence of large subsidiaries of American corporations on Canadian policy has become a source of criticism and friction. Similarly, the extensive circulation of American newspapers and magazines is seen as a threat to distinctive Canadian culture. On the other hand, the military security enjoyed by Canada through the working arrangements of the two military establishments is a great boon. And the interchange of people, through tourism and daily commuting across the joint border, knits the two nations in friendship. Finally, the history of a century and a half of peace between them has generated respect and mutual trust. Although Canada shows more inclination to enlightened patriotism than does the United States, the influence of its larger neighbor undoubtedly acts as somewhat of a brake on further movement in this direction.

Iceland is so tiny a country and one so isolated that its significance for the possible spread of enlightened patriotism is small. It ranked twenty-seventh in national support for world order (easily the lowest of the five Scandinavian nations) but its potentiality was higher—nineteenth. Iceland was an original member of the United Nations. It derives its security from membership in NATO, though here the United States plays the dominant protective role. As a peripheral member of NATO Iceland, like Norway and Denmark, understandably favors a stronger world order as a further protection.

Of the 18 European nations (excluding Turkey) in the first third of the total list of 114, we have discussed 13—Switzerland, Sweden, and 11 members of NATO. The remaining 5 European nations are Austria, Finland, Hungary, Ireland, and Yugoslavia. Only Hungary is a member of the Warsaw Pact. (Czechoslovakia has a potentiality for enlightened patriotism that falls just below the top third of the nations.)

Austria is more like Switzerland than any other country. After ten years of occupation by Allied troops following World War II, it became an independent state again by treaty. Immediately the Austrian parliament adopted a constitutional statute declaring the nation's permanent neutrality. It joined the United Nations as soon as an exception was granted to the requirement of participation in collective action against an aggressor. It was already a member of many specialized agencies. Austria has abstained on all U.N. votes on cold war issues. Like Geneva, Vienna has become host to U.N. agencies— UNESCO's European Coordinating Center for Social Sciences, the U.N. Industrial Development Organization, the U.N. Conference on the Peaceful Uses of Outer Space, and the U.N. Conference on the Law of Treaties. Austria has contributed troops to the U.N. peacekeeping operation in Zaire and on Cyprus, though it has a smaller military establishment than Switzerland.

Austria, though neutral, has carried on massive efforts to aid refugees from neighboring countries. In 1956 it sponsored the resolution in the U.N. General Assembly that proposed humanitarian aid to those who fled Hungary after the Soviet armed suppression of rebellion against the newly imposed government. Austria accepted two thousand of the refugees itself. It took the same stance and provided extensive aid in the similar Czech crisis of 1968. In table 1, Austria holds ninth rank in support for world order; and in table 4, it is tenth in potentiality for enlightened patriotism, ranking just below the Netherlands.

Finland is geographically squeezed between the Soviet Union and the NATO member, Norway, in perhaps the most precarious position in Europe. It has declared neutrality and has maintained cooperative relations both ways. Finland is an active collaborator in the Nordic Union but at the same time has special relations — exchange of scientists and extensive trade—with the Soviet Union. It is represented diplomatically in both East and West Germany. Finland entered the United Nations in 1955 but stays out of Great Power clashes in the General Assembly. It has been said that Finland plays the role of doctor rather than judge. It was one of the nine sponsors of the U.N. resolution promoting East-West collaboration in Europe. Finland was an elected member of the Security Council in 1969–70. Max Jacobson of Finland was a strong candidate for U.N. Secretary-General when Kurt Waldheim was selected. Finland has twice sent troops and has sent observers of cease-fires in U.N. peacekeeping missions five times.

In table 1, Finland holds twentieth rank on the NSWO index and is fifteenth in potentiality for enlightened patriotism. Its many attempts to act as an intermediary between East and West augment its service to world order. President Kekkonen was awarded the Nobel Peace Prize in 1975 in recognition of this contribution. Finland is clearly following in the footsteps of the pioneers.

Less can be said about Ireland. That nation is in a much more protected situation than Austria and Finland, but it has not failed to be supportive of world order. Active in U.N. matters, Ireland has sent peacekeeping forces eight times, including to the Middle East, Zaire, and Cyprus. It favors a European parliament in Strasbourg of both East and West that would succeed the Council of Europe. Ireland ranks twenty-second on the NSWO index and is twenty-third in potentiality for enlightened patriotism. Its position far below the pioneers is largely a result of lower scores in enlightenment and INGO participation. It is not as cosmopolitan a country as the smaller nations on the European continent. There is also the handicap of its preoccupation with the struggle between Catholics and Protestants in Northern Ireland. For these reasons, the majority of the Irish people are not likely to become enlightened patriots in the near future.

Yugoslavia is unique ideologically and geographically. In some ways its situation is like Finland's; in other ways quite different. During World War II, there were two "undergrounds" in Yugoslavia after the German conquest of the country: the partisans of the preexisting regime, the Chetniks, and the Communists led by Tito. They struggled against each other even as they both struggled against the Germans. Before the Soviet troops moved in to occupy the country in 1944–45, the Communists had won out. Until 1948, Yugoslavia continued as a satellite of the USSR, like the other Eastern European countries. In that year Tito was denounced by the Cominform for various heresies and his regime was subjected to a boycott. He withdrew Yugoslavia from COMECON (the bloc economic organization now called CEMA). It presently has economic relations with the Soviet bloc, the Western nations, and the People's Republic of China. Since the regime remains Communist, Yugoslavia is like Finland in reverse. Finland is also between the two blocs but remains ideologically sympathetic with the West. Yugoslavia was one of the leaders in attempting to form a nonaligned bloc which would become a potent third force in the United Nations. After some success in the late fifties, the movement petered out in the sixties. Yugoslavia joined the United Nations in 1945. It responded to U.N.

peacekeeping calls in Zaire and the Middle East. Though Yugoslavia is, like Finland, a genuine bridge between East and West, it is too occupied with domestic problems to devote much energy to world affairs. There are serious conflicts among the several nationalities that compose the country, and there is great anxiety about what will happen when Tito dies.

Yugoslavia holds twenty-eighth rank on support for world order and twenty-fourth on potentiality for enlightened patriotism. The prospects for the nation to improve its position do not seem bright.

Hungary, one of the participants in the Warsaw Pact that experienced a popular uprising against dominance by the Soviet Union (in 1956), has a higher NSWO score than the other pact members but is still fifty-first in national support for world order; it rises to thirty-fourth on potentiality. This is because of high scores on enlightenment, INGO participation, and urgency of trade. Its potentiality rank reflects its similarity before World War II to Western European nations, a similarity that has been lessened by the postwar situation.

Although the Hungarian Communist Party received only 17 percent of the votes in the election of 1947, it seized power and formed the Hungarian Peoples' Republic in 1949. Latent discontent became overt after Stalin's death in 1953 and a coalition government was established. But when, under President Nagy, it began to relax controls, the government was ousted by the Communist Party for anti-Marxism. In October 1956 discontent boiled over in Budapest and Nagy was restored to power by popular demand. The Soviet Union reacted immediately and sent troops that overwhelmed the defenders of the coalition government. Thousands of Nagy's supporters fled into exile. The repressive government that followed gradually relaxed its controls in the sixties, but its foreign policy continues to be dictated by the Soviet Union.

Like the other Soviet satellites, Hungary is a member of the Warsaw Pact Organization and of CEMA, the Communist economic community. It became a member of the United Nations and of some of the specialized agencies in 1955. It was also one of the group of small European nations that in 1965 sponsored a U.N. resolution calling for greater cooperation between Eastern and Western European nations. Although the nation's history suggests that many of its people would like to become nonaligned, like Austria, under present circumstances there is no likelihood that the government could become sufficiently autonomous to let the Hungarian people choose a course of enlightened patriotism.

Australia and New Zealand have such similar backgrounds, regimes, problems, and scores on the research indexes that they will be treated together. Both were members of the League of Nations and are charter members of the United Nations. Like the other countries of the British Commonwealth, they have participated actively in both the United Nations and the specialized agencies. New Zealand, has furnished U.N. peacekeeping forces more often than Australia—six times as opposed to five. Both were members of ANZUS (Australia, New Zealand, and the United States), a mutual security organization that was absorbed into the Southeast Asia Treaty Organization (SEATO). (Since the demise of SEATO, ANZUS is once again independent.) Both countries are interested in the fate of certain South Pacific Islands —Australia in Nauru and Papua, New Zealand in the Cook Islands. The two countries rank eighteen and nineteen on support for world order and are twelfth and fourteenth in potentiality for enlightened patriotism. Of the two, Australia seems less humanitarian in spirit. It has excluded prospective immigrants from the Orient and has not been as critical of apartheid in South Africa and Rhodesia as most European states. New Zealand has a better record and seems, therefore, more promising for the early development of enlightened patriotism.

Like West Germany, Japan has tried very hard since World War II to earn its way back into a position of world respect. Its military power is insignificant for a nation that is so large and industrialized—259,000 men in all branches of service. Japan

has renounced atomic weapons but is protected by a mutual
security treaty with the United States. It started joining the
specialized agencies in the late forties and was admitted to the
United Nations itself in 1956. It has worked consistently for
disarmament and peace and trades with all countries, including both the Soviet Union and the Peoples Republic of China.
Other nations in Asia worry about its economic power.

Japan ranks seventeenth in support for world order and
thirteenth in potentiality for enlightened patriotism. The uncertainty of the future relations between the two great Asian
powers, Japan and China, fosters equal uncertainty about
Japan's probable stance toward world order. If the two should
become hostile competitors for the favor of their neighbors,
they might become so selfishly preoccupied that neither would
worry about the welfare of the world. Though Japan has the
resources to make a great contribution to world peace, it cannot be counted on to move towards enlightened patriotism.

The five Latin American countries in table 4 are Mexico,
Chile, Brazil, Venezuela, and Colombia. All of the these are
near the end of the list—in ranks twenty-seven, twenty-eight,
thirty-one, thirty-two, and thirty-six. This level of potentiality
makes them unpromising candidates for enlightened patriotism in the near future. Mexico has great stability and has made
marked economic progress in recent years, but the level of
education among the rural half of its population is still low and
few of even the well-educated are in close touch with their
peers in other countries. President Echeverria did, however,
make a world tour in 1973 to demonstrate Mexico's friendship
with the Great Powers, both East and West. In *The Meeting of
East and West*, the philosopher F.C.S. Northrop named Mexico
as the country in which Occidental and Oriental cultural influences were most effectively fused, a fusion that perhaps
suggests a future role for Mexico as a leader toward world
unity.[3] It has already been a faithful supporter of the United
Nations and the specialized agencies as well as the Organization of American States.

Since 1970 Chile has been in constant turmoil and strife. The election of an avowed Communist, Salvador Allende Gossens, to the presidency in a threeway race in which he received a plurality, but not a majority, touched off a violent internal struggle. His government nationalized foreign corporations and many banks, though the left coalition did not control the parliament. In 1973 he was assassinated in a military coup. General Pinochet became the head of government and proclaimed that there would be no elections for at least five years. The uncompromising dictatorship now in power has destroyed the progressive and humane reputation Chile enjoyed under President Frei in the late sixties. The forces that might return Chile to the role of a good global citizen are suppressed and helpless.

Brazil, though under a dictator, has not gone through so traumatic an experience as Chile. Though it was the world's leading producer of coffee after World War II, a fall in the price brought severe economic hardship. From 1964 on there were political disorders culminating in rule by military leaders. Tight censorship of the press was instituted in 1972. Despite the eclipse of democratic government, the economy of Brazil has recently prospered. San Paolo has become one of the great industrial cities of the world. Brazil has traditionally been a firm supporter of international cooperation, being a prominent member of both the League of Nations and the United Nations. It has sent peacekeeping contingents to the Middle East, Zaire, and Cyprus. Its present internal political problems, however, do not augur well for increased support for world order.

Venezuela is the most prosperous nation in South America, largely because it is the fifth largest oil producer in the world. It has had a democratic regime since 1958 and, though pro-Western in foreign policy, it has had diplomatic relations with Communist countries and recognizes the Venezuelan Communist Party. Venezuela has tended not to recognize governments inaugurated by military coups. Like its neighbors, it has been a loyal member of the United Nations and the Organization of American States, but has been an underachiever in support for world order. Its ranks of forty-five on the NSWO index, and thirty-two on potentiality for enlightened patriotism do not suggest that Venezuela will soon follow in the pioneers' footsteps.

Colombia, at the thirty-sixth rank in potentiality, has a somewhat spotty record. Only in 1974 did fighting between leftist guerillas and government troops cease. In that year, a national election brought in a reformist president and constitutional government was resumed after twenty years. Colombia's U.N. record is excellent. It has served three terms on the Security Council and one of its citizens was the first Latin American president of the General Assembly. It has contributed peacekeeping troops three times. Colombia is also active in OAS and the Latin American Free Trade Association. It originated the idea of the Andean Development Corporation, in which Ecuador, Peru, and Bolivia are other participants. It was the first country to receive the United States Peace Corps. But its rank of thirty-eight on potentiality for enlightened patriotism is not good, probably because the nation is too poor to have a well-educated population.

The two Middle-Eastern countries, Kuwait and Iran, are in the upper third of the total list and have greater potential. Kuwait, to the surprise of all but the well informed, has the highest per capita gross national product in the world. A tiny country possessed of huge oil resources, it has grown from a population of some two hundred thousand to more than a million in ten years. Less than 20 percent of the people are natives; there are twice as many men as women. Though the government is a monarchy by the constitution of 1964, the rulers are elected for life. The system is modern but paternalistic. Public education is lavishly supported. Since the traditional elite from which the rulers come sees the future of the country as dependent on trade with all countries in the world, the foreign policy is supportive of the United Nations and of aid to underdeveloped countries. As an Arab nation, however, Kuwait is involved in the conflict with Israel; and, depending on the policies adopted by the Organization of Petroleum Exporting Countries, she may find herself subject to severe criticism from oil-consuming nations. These sources of possible hostility could embitter Kuwait and make the nation less interested in promoting world welfare than it was before 1973. Its fifth-ranked position on both support for world order and potentiality for enlightened patriotism might not continue. On the other hand, if the Arab-Israeli conflict is settled, and if the oil producers and consumers agree on price policies, Kuwait will be a prime candidate to join the pioneers. These "ifs" are large and difficult changes to effect, however.

At the time the research was done, Iran also made an impressive score on the NSWO index, ranking eleventh. At that time its predicted score was much lower, at rank forty-six. It was an outstanding overachiever, probably because of the Shah's ambitions for his country. In the last decade, however, Iran's wealth has grown by leaps and bounds as its oil resources were exploited and world petroleum prices rose. The Shah has been making strenuous efforts through education and the mass media to bring his subjects into the twentieth century. Probably Iran's high level of support for world order would not now appear as overachievement and its potentiality would be higher than twenty-fifth. Among the Middle-Eastern oil producers, Iran (like Saudi Arabia) has been successful in keeping cordial ties with Western countries while still adhering to OPEC policies. It is also friendly with the East Europeans. A conflict with Iraq over the treatment of the Iranian minority in Iraq has been settled, so that Iran now appears to have remarkably even-handed relations with most countries in the world. In that sense, its foreign policy appears enlightened. In so authoritarian a state, however, it seems likely that there will be more support for world order than for enlightened patriotism; the government can produce the former, but only the people can express the latter. And it will take much longer in large Iran than in small Kuwait for the people to become enlightened and participant in world affairs. For this reason, Iran is only marginally promising.

The last country to merit discussion is the Ivory Coast. Its rank of six on the NSWO index makes it also a great over-achiever, since its potentiality for enlightened patriotism is only at rank twenty-two. The Ivory Coast is similar to Iran in that a strong leader has decided that rapid modernization and peaceful relations with other countries are the right goals for the nation. Under President Houphouet-Boigny, the Ivory Coast has supported the United Nations and its specialized agencies. Houphouet-Boigny is a forceful but benevolent dictator who has maintained close ties with France and his neighbors (fellow French colonies until after World War II). He and the members of his administration are heavily dependent on foreign capital for their privileged position. Their paternal rule is not conducive to the development of enlightened patriotism. It will be some time before the nation's people will have the spirit of the pioneers.

I shall dismiss the remaining six nations. Lebanon, Egypt, and Israel have been so absorbed in the Arab-Israeli struggle as to make a humane world view for them practically impossible. Liberia is too much a client state of the United States to take independent initiative in foreign policy. The people of Pakistan, following the secession of Bangladesh, are too preoccupied with rebuilding their own nation to be concerned with anything so unselfish as the problems of the world at large. Earlier, Pakistan was able to supply a large contingent to the U.N. peacekeeping operation in West Irian. Morocco, at the forty-seventh rank in the NSWO index and holding the thirty-eighth rank in potentiality for enlightened patriotism, shows no promise either. Only in 1977 did King Hassan permit a parliamentary election, after seven years of dictatorship. Political conditions are still unstable, partly because of the controversy over the division of the former Spanish Sahara between Morocco and Mauretania, which is being challenged by Algerian rebels.

Of the thirty-four nonpioneer nations listed in table 4 as having potentiality for developing enlightened patriotism, the analysis shows only twenty to be at all promising. The comments made on each country demonstrate that there are influences other than those brought out in the original research that should be used in conjunction with the potentiality scores. I have attempted to gauge the degree of correction that needed to be applied to each score and have drawn up table 5 to express the combined result of the statistical and the qualitative data. The nations are arranged in descending order of potentiality. The smallest corrections have been made in the left column, moderate corrections in the middle column, and heavy corrections in the right column. The weights assigned to the qualitative data are, of course, subject to challenge. At least the table gives a concrete presentation to which criticism can be addressed.

If we consider the United States, the Soviet Union, the Peoples Republic of China, Japan, West Germany, and Britain as the Great Powers, the outlook as shown is not reassuring. None of them is a strong prospect to develop enlightened patriotism in the near future. Of the top five on the table, Austria and Finland are particularly significant. They both find themselves caught between the East and the West and therefore have a maximum interest in a firmer world order. Since they are model democracies, the spirit of enlightened patriotism is soon likely to match their support for world order. Even if one optimistically included the Netherlands, Luxemburg, New Zealand, Australia, Canada, Belgium, Britain, Japan, Italy, the German Federal Republic, Kuwait, Ireland, and Iceland as early possibilities for enlightened patriotism and added to them the four pioneers, the combined population of the nineteen nations would be only about 385 million. This is a mere 10 percent of the world's population. Prospects are improved if the power to change the world is measured by gross national product. Then the nineteen nations account for about 31 percent of world power—$1,260 billion out of more than $4,000 billion. This 31 percent would rise to more than 60 percent if the United States were to reach the level of enlightened patriotism now exemplified by the pioneers. The likelihood of such a drastic shift in the stance of the citizenry of the United States is, however, slim.

TABLE 5
Revised Estimates of Potentiality for
Enlightened Patriotism of Twenty Nations

Order of Scores Slightly Revised	All Scores Moderately Reduced and Order Slightly Revised	All Scores Heavily Reduced and Order Revised
Austria		
Netherlands		
Luxemburg		
Finland		
New Zealand		
	Australia	
	Canada	
	Belgium	West Germany
	Britain	Kuwait
	Japan	
	Italy	Iceland
Ireland		
Mexico		
	Yugoslavia	
		United States
		Ivory Coast
		Iran

It would be a mistake, nevertheless, to ignore the continuing changes that promise higher levels of support for world order. Global educational enrollments rose by 52 percent between 1960 and 1971 and the number of international non-governmental organizations grew by almost 55 percent. The similarity of these two rates of increase over roughly a decade is good evidence that changes in background variables are occurring rapidly, changes that my research suggests will foster the spread of enlightened patriotism to more countries.

From table 5, the most probable area for a cluster of nations motivated by enlightened patriotism is Western Europe. The pioneers are located there and five other nearby nations—Austria, Belgium, the Netherlands, Luxemburg, and Finland—are good prospects. Unfortunately the larger nations of Western Europe—West Germany, France, Italy, and Britain—seem unlikely to develop enlightened patriotism soon, even though they are fellow members of the European Community with Denmark, Netherlands, Belgium, and Luxemburg. The large countries do not feel the same urgency for a firm world order as the small ones. It appears that their governments will have to be pressured from within by groups committed to world order and imbued with a spirit of enlightened patriotism before they will adopt a global orientation.

6

The United Nations

The spread of enlightened patriotism is only one of the slender hopes for world order. Another is that the increase in multilateral diplomacy will foster a sense of common destiny among delegates to the meetings of U.N. agencies and regional institutions. The research of Chadwick Alger and one of his doctoral students, Gary Best, carried out at the United Nations headquarters in 1959 and 1960 reveals the basis for this hope.[1]

Alger first interviewed twenty-five delegates to the General Assembly during the first two weeks of their U.N. service (in the fourteenth session) and again near the end of that session. The delegates represented nations in the Far East, Middle East, Europe, Africa, and the Americas. Thirteen came directly from other foreign affairs posts; the remainder came from other governmental posts, from parliamentary service, or from private life. Alger found that the horizons of at least half of the delegates interviewed expanded markedly in the three months between interviews. Through their contacts they learned of countries and issues about which they had been totally ignorant. Delegates told how surprised they were at the positions taken on various issues by particular nations. This finding is borne out by the observation of two United States congressmen who earlier served as delegates to the General Assembly.

Many delegates coming from distant countries, relying on their own press and on diplomatic channels for their background information, frequently did not understand why the United States took the position it did on many issues. In a surprising number of instances, delegates altered their views on matters under discussion after acquiring additional background as a result of talks with representatives of the United States and other nations.[2]

A Western European delegate reported:

On my committee men come year after year, and friendly relations continue despite disagreement over policy. It is very important that people in international conferences know each other well. It permits the reaching of compromises. One has choices of many kinds of words for stating the same thing in either very polite or very rash words. Therefore, it is useful to have friends negotiating in international conferences.[3]

An African delegate credits face-to-face experience with helping him to realize that other delegates "are, after all, human beings."[4] A Norwegian parliamentarian serving as a delegate said: "I will go back with a clearer view of the fact that my nation belongs to the whole world."[5]

In 1960 (the 15th session) Alger's doctoral student, Gary Best, interviewed randomly selected members of permanent national missions to the United Nations. As part of the interview he asked seven questions on the comparison between diplomatic experience at the U.N. and in a national capital.[6] For each of these seven questions, the percent answering "much more" or "more" at the U.N. is given after the question in table 6.

Alger believes research on communication shows that the less information is channeled to particular persons in an organization, the less the differentiation of perceptions within

TABLE 6
Diplomatic Experience at the U.N.
Compared with a National Capital

	More or Much More at the U.N.
Contact with diplomats from other countries	86%
Likelihood of communicating orally with diplomats from other countries	84%
Likelihood of communicating with another delegate without regard to diplomatic rank	83%
Likelihood of having contacts with delegates from an unfriendly country	81%
Informality of relations with other representatives	82%
Ease of exchanging "off the record information"	67%
Importance of mission as a source of information	77%

the organization. The high percentages in table 6 would then suggest that messages are shared more broadly at the United Nations than in a national capital. Alger further believes that this tends to remove one of the causes of misunderstanding and conflict—differing perceptions of reality.[7]

In summary, Alger suggests that an international organization:

> . . . increases the number of intergovernmental linkages and provides a different milieu for contact. . . . The United Nations not only offers decision-making bodies, such as the Assembly and councils, but builds an intergovernmental society around a problem. . . . Thus, relations are conducted through a host of capillaries and less through a few main arteries. When a problem eventually reaches the public arena in the Assembly, the outcome will be importantly shaped by the nature of the integrated society that has developed around the issue.[8]

The main business of the United Nations is not, of course, to provide a setting for fruitful transnational contacts; its chief aims are to adopt policies and give them effect. Its record in these respects has been disappointing, but so complex a system cannot be dismissed as a failure so long as it is still evolving. I shall therefore review the promise of its activities for enhancing world order.

The League of Nations, the first attempt to establish a world body that would keep the peace, was founded in 1919 out of the terrible experience of World War I in which ten million combatants were killed. The League suspended its political operations with the outbreak of World War II in 1939. It had been unable to prevent the incursion of Japan into China, of Italy into Ethiopia, and of Germany into Austria and Czechoslovakia. This institution founded to secure world order had proved too weak to control nationalism.

Deaths in World War II were even more numerous than in World War I—at least eighteen million combatants. The victors resolved to try once more to create a world organization that could keep the peace. The United Nations Charter was approved by fifty nations at San Francisco in June 1945 and was ratified in October. This time, signatory nations took the view that the organization could not successfully coerce one of the Great Powers. Therefore, the victors—Britain, the Soviet Union, the United States, France, and China—were made permanent members of the Security Council and each was given a veto over council resolutions invoking collective security. Thus, continuing peace was to depend upon harmony among the Great Powers and the call for collective security measures by the Security Council against other powers that were declared aggressors. The first and only case in which collective security has been practiced was against North Korea after its 1950 attack on South Korea. This resolution was sanctioned only because the Soviet Union was, at the time, boycotting the Security Council and was not present to cast the veto that would have prevented United Nations' action against a member of the Communist bloc. It is not likely that any of the five permanent members of the council will again lose its veto under similar circumstances.

The Cold War between the signers of the Warsaw Pact and the members of NATO (beginning in 1948 and continuing unabatedly until the early sixties) destroyed any hope that the five permanent members of the Security Council could work harmoniously together; and only on issues weakly related to their national interests has the U.N. General Assembly (not the Security Council) been able to employ preventive diplomacy or to police a cease-fire by inserting armed contingents of volunteers in Indonesia, Kashmir, Zaire, Cyprus, and the Middle East. As was mentioned in chapter 4, most of the contingents have been volunteered by small and medium-sized nations anxious to see a stronger system of world order. Much of the credit for the peacekeeping that has been accomplished by the United Nations belongs to Dag Hammarskjold who, between 1953 and 1961, boldly broadened the role of the secretary-general in dealing with threatening situations. He also developed a "constituency" whose members saw peace-keeping as an appropriate role for the "middle powers"—the four continental Scandinavian nations, Ireland, Austria, New Zealand, and Canada. Most of these have established standby forces. (Other states that have contributed fighting forces twice or more are Brazil, Yugoslavia, India, Pakistan, and Indonesia.) The nations with standby forces prefer a U.N. as:

> . . . a physician to its troubled members, not a judge. Politically impartial, noncoercive peacekeeping is seen as an especially apt extension of these preferences for the U.N.-as-conciliator. Active intermediary efforts to control local conflicts, particularly if these raise the specter of big power competitive intervention, are viewed as supremely appropriate tasks for the U.N. to undertake and for these states to support, with political backing, with money, and if possible with manpower or other facilities.[9]

Middle powers are big enough to discharge significant responsibilities but not big enough for others to fear them.

The Nordic nations have passed legislation that not only establishes standby forces, but provides for their training together, despite the fact that Norway and Denmark are members of NATO but Sweden and Finland are not.

Although the disarmament committee has diligently tried to get agreement on steps toward disarmament, the two major military powers —the United States and the Soviet Union— have preferred to carry on their negotiations for a Strategic Arms Limitation Treaty bilaterally. Since for almost a decade the United States was fighting with South Vietnam and the Soviet Union was supporting North Vietnam, a veto of any attempt to bring the United Nations in as a party to the negotiations was a foregone conclusion. After the end of that war, however, the United Nations General Assembly voted to hold a special session on disarmament in May and June, 1978. Besides reaching broad agreement on the urgency of initiating a process of gradual, worldwide disarmament, the 149 member-states represented there decided to add several more Third World members to the United Nation Conference on Disarmament at Geneva and to establish a rotating chairmanship in place of the cochairmanship of the United States and the Soviet Union. The Tenth Special Session felt that the Assembly could not undertake positive steps until the conclusion of the negotiations on a Strategic Arms Limitation Treaty that were concurrently in progress between the United States and the Soviet Union (see p.1).

The United Nations has, however, seven peace-related accomplishments to its credit since the Korean War: the Antarctic Treaty of 1959 that prohibits any measure of a military nature there; the Treaty Banning Tests in the Atmosphere, in Outer Space and Under Water of 1963; the Treaty in Principles Governing the Activities of States in the Exploitation of Space, Including the Moon and Celestial Bodies, of 1967; the Treaty for the Prohibition of Nuclear Weapons in Latin America of 1967; the Treaty on Non-proliferation of Nuclear Weapons of 1968; the Treaty on the Prohibition of the Emplacement of Nuclear Weapons of Mass Destruction in the

Sea-bed and the Ocean Floor and in the Subsoil Thereof, of 1971; and the Convention on the Prohibition of the Development, Production, and Stockpiling of Bacteriological (Biological) and Toxic Weapons and on their Destruction, of 1972. Among the nuclear powers, the Soviet Union, the United States, and Great Britain have signed all seven pacts, as have many powers not possessing nuclear weapons. Some nations that have more recently acquired the capability of producing nuclear weapons have not, however, signed.

Until about 1958, the Western powers were dominant in the United Nations. They were able to line up a majority of votes on any issue that involved their vital interests. Their dominance sprang from several sources: the West European base of the League of Nations, the aid extended through the Marshall Plan by the United States to many nations after World War II, the postwar U.S. monopoly in atomic weapons, and the historical admiration of many countries for American democracy. With the Soviet achievement of an atomic bomb in 1948, a hydrogen bomb in 1953, and intercontinental missiles in 1957, the relative power of the Soviet bloc in the United Nations steadily increased. In the late fifties there emerged a nonaligned bloc, under the leadership of Prime Minister Nehru of India and Marshall Tito of Yugoslavia, that strove to gain power by playing the Western and the Communist blocs against each other. The nonaligned nations were only partially successful in this effort. It was not until decolonization gained momentum in the early sixties that the two Cold War blocs found themselves outvoted in the U.N. General Assembly by new members. From 59 nations at the end of 1959, the United Nations grew to a membership of 126 by the end of 1969. By then the Third World could dominate the U.N. on issues like South African apartheid and "a new economic order"—issues on which these nations felt strongly.

Meanwhile the relations between the Soviet Union and the People's Republic of China began to deteriorate. At the end of World War II the Soviet Union had given military aid to Mao's partisans until they conquered mainland China and expelled the forces of Chiang Kai-Shek to Taiwan. Thereafter, Soviet support continued by many means, particularly by supplying technicians to build up Chinese industry. All this changed in 1960 when, because of ideological differences, tension mounted between the two nations. The Soviet technicians were withdrawn. This split in the Communist ranks fueled rivalry of the two for world leadership of the Communist movement. Perhaps this made the Soviet Union less confident in its struggle against the United States. In any event, the Cold War gradually became less acrimonious and finally reached a level of détente in 1972 as the United States was withdrawing its forces from Vietnam.

During the same period, the attitude of the United States toward China was softening. After twenty-two years of voting against China's admission to the United Nations, the United States switched to its support in 1971. Since then, the United States has had better relations with both China and the Soviet Union than they have had with each other. Though there are now three ideological rivalries among the permanent members of the Security Council—between the three Western powers (Britain, France, and the United States) and the Soviet Union, between the Western powers and China, and between the Soviet Union and China—none of the three is as fraught with global danger as was the Cold War of the fifties. This reduction in tension has been achieved by diplomacy operating under changed conditions, not appreciably by the efforts of the United Nations. Nor is one to conclude that nations are dropping their guard. In 1970, world military expenditures exceeded the total income of the poorest half of humanity.[10]

The United Nations has been criticized for inefficient administration almost from the beginning. This is not surprising. Its large secretariat is drawn from many nations with differing cultures and differing extents of administrative experience. The influx of representatives from developing nations after 1959 has added to the organizational problems. It is hard to achieve both geographical representation of all areas of the world and a high level of knowledge and skill in the secretariat. The secretary-general who presides over the operations of the United Nations is in the unenviable position of having to combine devotion to the organization's aims (as set forth in the charter) with a political skill that will keep 149 nations happy with his staff appointments.

Currently, the developing countries are exulting in their newly developed power in the United Nations; while the developed countries feel aggrieved by their loss of dominance. There is talk of withdrawal from the U.N. by some of the main contributors to the budget if the policies adopted are inimical to their interests. Since the main bone of contention is the gap between the developed and the developing countries, the field of struggle is moving from security affairs to economic and social affairs. To achieve cooperation in these fields was an original, basic task of the United Nations. It was to supervise this work that the U.N. Economic and Social Council was created. The detailed performance of these tasks is the job of the autonomous specialized agencies, of which there are now fifteen. Thus, their operations take on added significance.

A very complex question is whether the United Nations is gaining or losing support among its members. A careful canvass of this matter has been made by Edward Thomas Rowe.[11] One measure he uses is the amount of pecuniary support given to institutions of the U.N. system by member governments. Expenditures in dollars rose from 173 million annually in the years 1946–50 to 1,146 million in the year 1970–71. At first glance this seems to be a great increase in commitment, but after allowance is made for inflation and the much larger U.N. membership (though it is true that late comers are disproportionately small and poor), the increased commitment of particular nations turns out to be modest. It is reassuring, however, to learn that the commitment is equivalent to a higher proportion of each country's military budget. Perhaps even more significant is that two-thirds of the 1970–71 budget was devoted to the developing countries, a strikingly higher proportion than in the early days. Thus, the commitment appears to be more unselfish.

Rowe finds that the wealthier states have been more regular in voting on issues in all periods, probably because the others cannot afford adequate representation in all the U.N. institutions to which they belong. In general, however, it is Rowe's conclusion that the developing nations and the smaller developed ones are showing keener interest in, and commitment to, the United Nations than the larger developed nations. He believes (at least through 1971, the date of his study), that this commitment is growing. Both the United States and the Soviet Union seem to be less committed. Rowe concludes that the United Nations has more vitality than the superpowers believe.

The specialized agencies may be put into three groups. One contains organizations of a highly specialized and technical sort that have small budgets —the Universal Postal Union, the International Telecommunications Union, the World Meteorological Organization, the International Civil Aviation Organization, and the International Maritime Consultative Organization.

A second group has to do with international financial and commercial arrangements—the International Bank for Reconstruction and Development (World Bank), its two associated agencies, the International Development Agency and the International Finance Corporation, the International Monetary Fund, and the General Agreement on Tariffs and Trade. These five specialized agencies carry on the operations sanctioned by their charters with less supervisory coordination from the United Nations than the other ten agencies. The functions of the first four are significant to the growth of world order mainly for the contribution they make to overcoming the dissatisfaction of developing countries with their role in the world system. This problem will be discussed below.

The third group of agencies works more closely with the United Nations itself, under the supervision of the Economic and Social Council (ECOSOC). The oldest of all the specialized agencies, the International Labour Organization, was established in 1919 under the League of Nations. The other three were established after World War II.

The purpose of the International Labour Organization is to improve the lot of workers around the world by securing adherence of its member nations to international conventions on working conditions, collective bargaining procedures, human rights, and the like. Until World War II, its members were chiefly industrialized countries. It experienced only moderate success, but adherence to the conventions it adopted occurred mainly in these developed countries. With the great flood of new members from the Third World after decolonization, the ILO's field of operation became more differentiated. The institution's success among the developing nations depends largely on whether the convention can be effected cheaply, and whether the country has sufficient know-how to administer it efficiently. The field of human rights, like freedom of association, is one in which these requisites can be met, and it is in this field that the ILO has had the greatest influence on the developing nations.[12]

The International Labour Organization is making a contribution to the achievement of world order, but not a striking one. One circumstance that handicaps it is the charter provision for tripartite national delegations representing employers, workers, and governments. This structure was adopted when the Soviet Union was the only member with a Communist government. Now employer representatives from capitalist countries complain that those from the Communist states selected to fill the employer role are, in fact, governmental representatives, giving the governments overrepresentation in the conference as a whole.[13] This makes for quarrels within the organization, and it is the chief reason that the United States withdrew from the ILO in 1977.

The World Health Organization has been generally noncontroversial and has been regarded as making significant contributions to world welfare. Its help, especially to developing countries, has been appreciated; and, to the degree that it symbolizes cooperation and humanitarian concern on the part of the developed countries, it has probably strengthened world order. Since it has been performing its services for almost thirty years, it has found a secure niche in the global system; but is unlikely to become a greater support for world order than it already is.

The Food and Agriculture Organization is now heavily involved in the new United Nations effort to combat world hunger. Its role in that new program will be discussed later.

UNESCO, the United Nations Educational, Scientific, and Cultural Organization, is perhaps the most famous of the specialized agencies. This may be because its greatest emphasis has been on education, a field of effort that holds out hope both for personal achievement and societal development. UNESCO has sought to improve education in many ways: by sending experts to give advice on curriculum, teaching methods, and school administration to authorities in the less developed world; by providing fellowships for graduate training abroad; by organizing regional conferences on many subjects for schoolmen; by carrying on a world campaign to eliminate illiteracy; by operating an educational clearinghouse to supply up-to-date information on educational practices; and by publishing worldwide statistics on education.

Since we have found that the more enlightened nations tend to support world order, we can assume that an institution like UNESCO that fosters education is making some contribution to world peace. Any such contribution will be made, however, at a glacial pace, since the ex-colonial countries cannot afford to expand schooling rapidly.

UNESCO has been making worthy contributions in the fields of science and culture, too. For instance, studies aimed at increasing food production from the seas and in the arid regions of the earth are of great significance to combating malnutrition. Very different services of lasting value are the preservation of historic monuments (like the temples on the Nile threatened by waters behind the Aswan High Dam) and the encouragement of translations into many languages of great literary works. But such activities contribute only indirectly and in the long run to a firmer world order. They contribute to material and spiritual welfare, but not in a way that directly emphasizes the interdependence of peoples.

A relatively new development among social scientists, and one in which UNESCO is much interested, is peace research. This differs from traditional political science in that economic, sociological, and psychological analyses are joined to political analysis. This scientific movement has become established since 1955. In those parts of the world in which the social sciences are well grounded, many capable investigators are involved, but there have been no great achievements as yet. Decisions on war and peace flow from the interaction of so many variables that even computer analysis has been unable to ferret out convincing chains of explanation.[14]

In December 1972 the General Assembly approved the establishment of a new institution, the United Nations University, and a year later adopted a charter for it. This university is described not as an intergovernmental organization like the specialized agencies, but as "a system of academic institutions." The headquarters, a programming and coordinating center, is located in Tokyo. The allied institutions are to form a decentralized system, integrated into the world university community. The system's missions are action-oriented research into the pressing global problems of human survival, development and welfare, and the post-graduate training of young scholars and research workers for the benefit of the world community. Presumably the allied institutions will mainly be departments or divisions of universities around the world that are qualified and eager to perform the two missions.

A hopeful development in the United Nations during the first half of the seventies was a noteworthy increase in U.N. efforts to wrestle with critical problems that confront humanity. One of the evidences of this trend was the convening of four world conferences — on the law of the sea, the human environment, world population, and food — and a Special Session of the General Assembly on a New Economic Order. In these conferences, the emphasis was on the impossibility of attacking these problems by separate national efforts, because each of them involves transnational relationships or flows. As an example, population growth is no longer merely a national problem: high rates of natural increase mean more mouths to feed, and food is running short not only in the countries where population is exploding, but in low-growth countries accustomed to importing food; secondly, rapid population increase in the absence of opportunities for emigration threatens to drive nations to invade the territory of others to find living space.

Leadership in this effort to bring the capabilities and resources of the United Nations to bear on crucial world problems has been mainly assumed by secondary powers, like Sweden, Canada, and Japan. They are seeking to have the United Nations clarify the existing status of each problem and then promote cooperative action. If the U.N. efforts were to bear fruits, even though slowly, the prestige of the organization would be greatly enhanced.

I shall first take up the dual problem of population and hunger. At first glance it seems simple to solve because we can clearly see what needs to be done. There would be little hunger were it not for the population explosion, and the population explosion would be no problem if much more food could miraculously be produced. It is an overwhelming problem simply because we do not know how to produce and distribute the food, or how to encourage enough people to limit human births.

This problem may be as old as humanity. Certainly since the early days of agriculture there have been recurrent famines as crops were scorched by the sun, devoured by locusts, or withered by shortage of water. The most famous commentary on the problem is by Thomas Robert Malthus, the English parson, who as a young curate and fellow of Jesus College, Cambridge, published in 1798 *An Essay on the Principle of Population*. His basic point was that "the power of population is indefinitely greater than the power in the earth to produce subsistence for men;" this because food increases only in arithmetic ratio while population, when unchecked, increases in geometric ratio. He saw misery, vice, and high mortality as inevitable consequences. Though there was abundant misery in the early years of the industrial revolution, the countries of Western Europe seemed to confound Malthus' gloomy view of the future: the productivity of agriculture kept up with, and even outdistanced, the growth in population. For more than a century few in the West worried about Malthus' prediction, particularly because birth control gradually came to be widely practiced. It is only since the introduction of modern medicine into the less developed countries, causing death rates to drop and rates of natural increase to become astronomical, that the Malthusian specter has been reborn. Although birth rates in Europe and North America are dropping to the level of population replacement, in the rest of the world the population explosion continues; efforts to halt it through programs of education in family planning and the provision of birth control devices are having minimal success. That the world population doubled from two to four billion between 1930 and 1976 is ominous.

Except for occasional famines because of disastrous harvests in countries that could not afford to purchase enough food from abroad, the production of agriculture seemed to be keeping pace with population needs until the late sixties. Indeed, until then the United States had tremendous surpluses of grain that had to be carried over from year to year. But in 1972, harvests were poor throughout the world. Cereal production fell by 20 percent. Suddenly there was the threat of widespread starvation. Bangladesh, Ethiopia, and sub-Saharan Africa were particularly hard hit. Though harvests have been better since 1972, many persons have starved in the meantime and few reserves have been accumulated. It is no longer fashionable to sneer at Malthus. History is verifying his prediction.

There is worldwide concern about both facets of the dual

problem. In August 1974, the United Nations convened a World Population Conference in Bucharest, Romania, attended by representatives of 137 nations. Shortly thereafter, in November, a World Food Conference was held in Rome under the auspices of the Food and Agriculture Organization of the United Nations. Representatives of 132 nations attended. Each conference aimed to bring together those most knowledgeable about the research on its aspect of the dual problem, so that the conference could forecast short-term developments, identify the serious subproblems, and canvass possible solutions. Since many of those present represented governmental bureaucracies, like census bureaus and departments of agriculture, the studies made by thousands of individual scientists could only be represented secondhand.

The research results funneled into the population conference stemmed from the labors of many kinds of specialists: demographers, economists, sociologists, anthropologists, social workers, experts in public health, geneticists, physiologists, and gynecologists. Three broad topics seemed to stand out: trends in births and deaths in all parts of the world, analysis of the determinants of fertility rates, and degree of success of programs of family planning.

Most of the demographic research originates in some 150 population centers around the world and is listed by the Committee for International Coordination of National Research in Demography.[15] Of these centers, 6 are supported by the U.N. Fund for Population Activities, 55 by governments, 64 by universities, and the remainder by other means. Ninety-four centers were conducting studies of differential fertility rates, their causes and their consequences, studies of birth control methods and their success and of attitudes toward population problems of various sectors of the population. They were not doing research on family planning. The remaining 57 centers may have been doing some of these kinds of research but they were distinctive in that they were carrying out evaluations of family planning programs, either their own or those launched by other agencies. There was particular interest in the various kinds of contraception and in the methods used to inform families about them.

Those carrying on research in these many centers are in touch with one another through findings published in scientific journals and through the rather thin web of scientific organizations. (The 1974–75 edition of the *Yearbook of International Organizations* lists only eight organizations, besides the U.N. Population Commission, devoted specifically to population matters.) Periodically there are international congresses that give opportunity for personal contacts. The International Union for the Scientific Study of Population serves as the focus for the demographers. The International Planned Parenthood Federation plays a somewhat less focal role for the family planners.

The evidence presented at the population conference for the need of collective action was so convincing that a World Population Plan of Action was adopted by acclamation. Whether these representatives can persuade their nations to pursue the objectives set forth remains to be seen.

The scientific backdrop of the food conference in Rome consisted of studies on all aspects of the world problem—the trends in food production, in price, in arable land and fertilizers available, in rate of adoption of more productive genetic strains, in assistance to the developing countries, in income to purchase food, and in levels of nutrition.

Hunger has been the subject of extensive research for a much longer period than population, and it has involved many more specialists of one sort or another. There are 118 organizations listed in the 1974–75 *Yearbook of International Organizations* whose activities are closely related to the problem of hunger. There is no convenient list of research centers in this case because thousands of departments of universities are carrying on studies in the different fields that bear on food production, from the genetics of edible plants and animals to the engineering of irrigation systems and the marketing and distribution of food for consumption. Perhaps the greatest effort of all goes into studies by biologists and chemists on methods of increasing yields in agriculture and animal husbandry.

The so-called green revolution testifies to the success of much of this research, though some experts are beginning to worry about the risk of concentrating production on a few genetic strains that might become vulnerable to novel parasitic organisms. In any case, there is great and intelligent effort to contribute to the solution of world hunger.

There is one sharp difference between the two aspects of the problem: the degree of resistance to proposed solutions. Food is in short supply and everyone is eager to have enough of it. Hence, there is consensus on the need for increasing the supply and an openness to rational and equitable plans for its distribution. Not so with the population side of the equation. Some nations and some religious bodies have, in the past, favored high rates of natural increase as a weapon in a struggle for dominance. In many countries children are considered as insurance for support in old age, and there is, therefore, opposition to birth control. For some religious groups there is a moral ban on all artificial methods of birth control as being unnatural and sinful. More generally, there is a feeling that decisions about having children are the exclusive prerogative of husbands and wives, and that privacy in this matter should be protected.

Despite the widespread resistance to birth control, in Asia, at least, governments have gone beyond merely educative efforts in family planning. For several years a number of countries have been facilitating birth control by the establishment of centers or camps for mass voluntary sterilization by vasectomy or tubal ligation. In a few instances, incentives like a small payment or a tax reduction are offered for acceptance of sterilization. Disincentives, like higher hospital fees for childbirth or tax increases after three children, are sometimes imposed.

From the point of view of world order, work on the population-hunger problem will be significant in several ways. First, if progress is made and anxieties eased, there should be less envy among nations and less strain in their relationships. Second, the general public in many nations will gradually become aware of the application of scientific results to the solving of the population-hunger problem. This should increase humanity's sense of one world, especially in nations afflicted with famine. Finally, as I shall emphasize in chapter 8, the continuing cooperation of experts in the twin aspects of this dual problem will contribute to a strengthening of the web of cooperation among nations.

Scientists have long realized the threats to the earth's biosphere entailed in many human practices and industrial processes, but the public has appreciated the extent of pollution and the manifold forms it takes only recently. The United Nations Conference on the Human Environment, held in Stockholm in 1972, was the first global attempt to evaluate the seriousness of the problems and to canvass the possible ways of dealing with them. Despite the absence of members of the Communist bloc (because the German Democratic Republic was not invited), 113 nations attended. The three main committees dealt with the assessment of environmental hazards, environmental management, and measures supporting assessment and management. The preparations were thorough, so that at the end of the twelfth day it was possible to adopt an Action Plan for the Human Environment. It was agreed that, although local and national governments would bear the chief responsibility for policy and action within their jurisdictions, there is need for international cooperation, both because many problems are becoming regional and global, and because developing countries will need pecuniary help to deal with them. One feature of the plan is the establishment of a global Earthwatch that includes research, monitoring, and the exchange of information about environmental problems. A large number of recommendations for planning environmental management were approved. They went beyond the control of pollution to the fostering of positive processes, such as preserving genetic diversity and crop breeding. The report gives great emphasis to the need for environmental education and public information. One of its striking features is the extent to which it connects environmental problems with broader questions of human rights, population policy, exhaustion of natural resources, economic development, and national sovereignty. The conference recommended that the U.N. General Assembly establish a governing council for environmental programs, a small secretariat, a voluntary fund for environmental programs, and a coordinating board to dovetail the work of the several U.N. agencies whose fields of activity are relevant. In 1973 the U.N. General Assembly adopted the Action Plan for the Human Environment, established the Council for Environmental Programs, set June 5 of each year as World Environment Day, and requested the secretariat to inform the Assembly when the furtherance of the action plan required a second conference.

Those U.N. initiatives, if pursued, may well be of great help in the building of world order. Cross-national pollution is already causing conflict in the world and presages more. The occurrence of "acid rain" in countries far removed from the source of air pollution has already sparked recrimination in Norway and Sweden against Germany. The misuse of the common environment today closely parallels the misuse of the grazing "commons" in English villages during the seventeenth and eighteenth centuries. Then, everybody's property turned out to be nobody's property because each herder was tempted to add sheep to his flock, the pastures became overgrazed, and the whole system had to be abandoned. Where sheep were the victims then, humans are the victims now.

One aspect of pollution, that of the oceans, is being dealt with by another conference. This is the United Nations

Third Conference on the Law of the Sea. The chief responsibility of its third committee is the preservation of the
marine environment. It is thus charged with ways and means
to control pollution. The committee is expected to recom-
mend national, regional, and global measures of control.
Two new aspects of this problem are the prevention of oil
spills from supertankers and the regulation of the disposal
of radioactive wastes.

The third conference as a whole has been meeting periodically since December 1973. The latest of seven sessions, each
lasting some two months adjourned September 14, 1978. The
conference, comprising 145 nations, is struggling to reach
consensus on a law of the sea convention. As a means to this
end it authored a *Single Negotiating Text* at the close of its third
session (Geneva, 1975) which became a *Revised Single Negotiating Text* during the fourth session (New York, 1976) and an
Informal Composite Negotiating Text at the end of the sixth session
(New York, 1977).

The work of the conference has been carried out in three
committees. The greatest progress has been made by the third
committee, which has dealt with the preservation and protection of the marine environment and with marine research. On
the latter subject there has been disagreement over the extent
to which coastal states should be permitted to control research
in their proposed exclusive economic zones. Scientists tend to
believe that research should be open to all states, at least up to
the edge of the territorial sea which now extends twelve miles
from shore. Nationalistic states want control of research to the
limit of their proposed exclusive economic zone, 200 miles
out.

The second committee has been dealing with the traditional
concerns of the Law of the Sea—the rights of navigation, the
breadth of the territorial sea, fishing rights, and the like.
Though there are still unsettled questions here such as
whether to give landlocked states rights in the exclusive
economic zones of coastal states, and how to set the outer limits

of the continental margin, the second committee has reached tentative agreement on several crucial matters.

The first committee was assigned the task of formulating regulations for the exploitation of the seabed and its subsoil. This is the most difficult task undertaken by the conference and any ensuing decisions may prove devisive. The developed nations want the opportunity to exploit widely (and quickly) the rich resources of cobalt, manganese, nickel, copper, and aluminum (often in the form of nodules resting on the ocean floor), governed only by very general rules. The developing nations, on the other hand, want the ocean floor beyond the exclusive national zone treated as the common property of mankind. To this end, the *Informal Composite Negotiating Text* proposes an International Seabed Authority which shall have exclusive jurisdiction beyond national jurisdictions. This authority would be governed by an assembly (one state, one vote) and an elected council, and would have a secretariat. The developed countries want the council to dominate the affairs of the authority; the developing countries would like the assembly to do so. The present text establishes an International Seabed Enterprise to carry on operations in the international zone under the authority. It also allows the International Seabed Authority to permit states and national, regional, or international enterprises to carry on operations under its control and supervision. The rules would be drawn so as to carry out the principle that the resources are the common heritage of mankind. What this provision is to mean in practice is still unclear. The present text does specify, however, that states or other juridical entities that contract with the authority to mine the seabed shall pay royalties into a special fund that will be distributed equitably among the member-states. The remaining disagreement between developed and developing countries is over the conditions and procedures under which the Seabed Authority may allow an agency other than the International Seabed Enterprise to carry on deep-sea mining.

There has been careful attention to the settlement of disputes in a proposal for a Law of the Sea Tribunal. There is growing consensus on the need for the tribunal but there is disagreement about the kinds of issues over which it should have jurisdiction.[16] The third report to the Club of Rome, *Reshaping the International Order*, suggests that traditional territorial sovereignty [in the seas] should be replaced by the concept of *functional* sovereignty, distinguishing jurisdiction over geographic space from sovereignty over specific usage. Functional sovereignty would permit the interweaving of national jurisdiction and international competence within the same territorial space, allowing the concept of the common heritage of mankind to be applied both within and beyond the limits of national jurisdiction.[17]

Though it is possible that the Law of the Sea Conference will ultimately fail, the participants are moderately hopeful that the obstacles remaining can be overcome. It is even possible that a final session in 1979 will be able to finish the job begun in 1973. If the nations do manage to adopt a convention that finds global acceptance, it will be humanity's greatest international achievement thus far.

The last current U.N. problem I shall consider came to the world's attention about 1960, after many former colonies attained independence. These developing nations perceived the General Agreement on Tariffs and Trade and the U.N. financial agencies (World Bank, IMF, IDA, and IFC) as being dominated by the developed countries and operated largely in their interest, thus imposing neocolonialism on the developing countries. The gap between the developed and developing countries was not narrowing despite programs of bilateral and multilateral aid.

In 1964, the developing nations demanded and got a United Nations Conference on Trade and Development (UNCTAD), operating as an organ of the General Assembly though not as a specialized agency. In 1972, UNCTAD passed a resolution urging the adoption of norms to govern international economic relations and calling for the formulation of a charter that would protect the rights of all countries, particularly the developing ones. On January 15, 1975, the General Assembly adopted the Charter of Economic Rights and Duties of States. This document expressed the position of the developing countries. Upon its adoption, the General Assembly set its seventh special session for September 1975 to attempt to establish "a new economic order." At 3:50 A.M. on September 16, 1975 the Assembly, after two weeks of seemingly hopeless deadlock between the developed and the developing nations, found a formula that enabled it to pass unanimously Resolution 3362. The seven sections of this complex resolution deal mainly with measures to improve agricultural productivity in the developing countries, hasten industrialization, and increase foreign trade.

Strengthening the scientific and technological infrastructure of agriculture in the developing countries is one of the resolution's goals. Both the U.N. Food and Agriculture Organization and the developed countries are asked to help. In particular, attention is called to the need to prevent postharvest losses in crops. Also stressed are the needs for food reserves to protect the underdeveloped nations in years of drought and for an early warning system to alert threatened countries when shortages are imminent.

Similar concern is shown for industrial production. The developing countries have felt that the developed countries have handicapped them by withholding information on business methods and refusing them access to modern technology. The resolution calls for acceleration of technological transfer and asks seven U.N. agencies to help in the process, particularly the Industrial Development Organization. In addition, it suggests that the developed countries create "intermediate technology" geared to the resources and capabilities of the developing countries. Another suggestion is that industries that are less competitive internationally be redeployed from the developed countries, so as to use available labor in the developing countries.

To make possible these advances in agriculture and industry, the resolution promises to ease the capital problems of the developing nations. One section sets a target of seven-tenths of 1 percent of the GNP of each developed country to be transferred, each year of the seventies, to the developing countries through bilateral or multilateral means. There are also plans for special "drawing rights" on the International Monetary Fund, increasing the capital of the World Bank Group, added national contributions to the U.N. Special Fund, and access to the capital markets of the developed nations.

Finally, there are stipulations about international trade. The main objective is the reduction of tariff and nontariff barriers against the exports of the developing countries so as to expand and diversify their trade in agricultural, semi-processed, and fully manufactured products.

The general aim of the resolution is clear: to benefit the developing nations by enlisting the help of the developed nations and the United Nations machinery. It is difficult to foresee its effectiveness. No developed nation can be forced to act in the manner set forth, but many of them have shown genuine support on a number of points. Shortly after the September 1975 agreement on Resolution 3362, a twenty-seven-nation Conference on International Economic Cooperation and Development was set up that included eight developed nations and nineteen developing nations. Over a period of eighteen months the members discussed the various points of the resolution, but at a meeting in Paris ending June 2, 1977, the developed nations refused to grant a blanket moratorium on $200 billion in debts owed by the Third World nations, and there was continuing disagreement over the establishment of an energy panel that would include oil-producing and oil-consuming nations.

U.N. conferences on global problems such as the five discussed above, scheduled at least two years in advance to allow expert preparation and attended by delegates from most nations of the world, have already set a pattern that is continuing as new world issues arise. It is too soon to judge the effectiveness of such conferences in meeting the needs that gave rise to them, though there are critics who see them as a generally ineffectual expenditure of time, energy, and money. Boyce Rensberger, a *New York Times* correspondent reacting to this criticism after attending the 1977 Conference on Desertification in Nairobi, makes three points worth pondering. First, he says that "United Nations world conferences have indeed catalyzed movements that . . . are essential if mankind is to cope with the myriad of problems beginning to degrade the quality of life almost everywhere."[18] As an example, he claims that in the past only the developed nations were concerned about the human environment; the 1972 Stockholm conference, however, convinced the developing countries that the resources of the biosphere must be carefully husbanded if there is to be any hope of improved standards of living. He also cites the fact that Mexico, long officially opposed to programs of family planning, became their supporter after attending the population conference in Bucharest. Second, Mr. Rensberger points out that these conferences have given world status to experts in several fields, which in turn has invigorated the national will to cope with the problems. Third, "by allying national efforts with a formally recognized international cause, many countries find it easier to mobilize financial and intellectual resources that might otherwise be diverted to less urgent matters."[19]

There are two economic problems related to the plight of the developing nations that the United Nations has not yet addressed seriously. These are the operations of multinational corporations or enterprises, and the equitable access of all nations to scarce natural resouces.

In the preceding pages, I have emphasized the great contributions that scientists of many kinds have made to the attack on global problems. I did not, however, report the help that INGOs, scientific and other, have made in the early stages of problem consideration. Actually, in fields as diverse as international trade, human rights, and technical assistance, INGOs with consultative status have assisted by calling attention to problems, helping to obtain needed data on them, making policy proposals, and participating, when asked, in discussion looking toward solutions. The approximately six hundred organizations currently enjoying consultative status with the Economic and Social Council or one of the specialized agencies constitute a rich resource for the United Nations when it confronts new problems, such as the two that I shall now broach.

One of the chief reasons for the demanding stance of the developing countries is their disappointment with the way multinational corporations have operated. These industrial and commercial giants, incorporated in developed countries and with subsidiaries located elsewhere, were originally seen by developing nations as a boon. The rapidity of their recent growth testifies to the need that has been felt for their services. Their total annual sales are now greater than the gross national product of any single country, with the exception of the United States and the Soviet Union. In 1971, the product of General Motors, at 28 billion dollars, was greater than the GNP of all but seventeen countries. Ten other multinationals topped 7 billion, the tenth of them having a GNP greater than Egypt (ranking thirty-eighth among the nations). In 1971, the investment of the U.S. multinationals was roughly 80 billion dollars; investments of European countries totaled about 22 billion, while Japan's was 4 billion.[20]

Multinationals have to obtain permission of the government of any country in which they do business, and are, of course, subject to the laws and taxes of that country. As explained above, the host country expects to reap benefits from their operations. The home government of the corporation expects their citizen stockholders to benefit, also; and, indirectly through taxation on incomes, the government itself expects a return. Generally speaking, all parties do in fact benefit in the early years of the relationship, but criticisms have tended to increase with time.

First, blue collar workers of the host country begin to feel the pinch of unemployment as labor-saving machinery is brought in for efficiency. Because the multinationals in retail business advertise lavishly, the host population sometimes is tempted to buy goods they have not had before and to skimp on necessities. The feeling of the workers, that they are not really improving their lot, is increased by awareness of the high standard of living of the foreign managers residing locally. Before long, the workers learn that a large share of the profits from local operations (52 percent in the average case) goes out of the country. A smaller proportion goes into local capital investment. The wealthier natives perhaps benefit from buying stock in the corporation, but the level of living of the poorer people is little changed. Thus it is that the ordinary citizens begin to feel exploited and to demand that their governments raise the corporation's taxes, impose new controls, or nationalize the operation altogether.

It must be said, however, that some multinationals have adopted policies of training local personnel for positions of management and encouraging local investment in the corporation. It is their aim to turn over the management responsibilities of the subsidiary to natives as rapidly as possible, cultivating a sense of identification of the host country with the multinational. It is difficult, however, to achieve this when the aims and plans of the corporation are global, while the host country's aspirations for the subsidiary are national. A similar disjunction between the corporation and the host country arises when the subsidiary expands into fields of operation not part of the original plan and not compatible with national plans.

Even the home government may feel aggrieved, particularly if an industrial multinational switches some of its operations from one foreign country to another so as to minimize the taxation at home. Labor unions in the home country are also placed at a disadvantage when such a corporation shifts home country operations to sites abroad. Since it is usually impossible to include the foreign workers in the same union with the home country workers, the latter have no effective protection from low wage competition.

For all these reasons, there is demand for multinational corporations to be more closely controlled. The parties who are satisfied with the present situation are the stockholders, the managers, the white collar workers who are well paid, and the host country firms that do a profitable business with the subsidiary. Both home and host governments and the ordinary citizens of both countries have occasion to complain.

There is another side, however, to the whole matter of multinational corporations. They bring in the capital, the technology, and the skills to run complex business organizations that can supply local economic needs efficiently. Originally, the developing countries regarded the multinationals as demonstrators of what could be done. They hoped that their people would acquire the skills and raise the capital to establish enterprises that would, in time, compete with and displace the foreign-based enterprises. It was expected that for a decade or more the managers of the multinationals would have to be drawn from the home country, but it was hoped that more and more of the personnel, over time, would be natives of the developing country.

Multinationals are welcomed by some students of world affairs because they are challenging the age-old authority of the national state. Since the advent of agriculture brought continuous territorial settlement of populations, the authority of the state over the activities of its inhabitants has been accepted. The multinational corporation, however, weakens the principle. Powerful economic units that move from country to country to take advantage of favorable conditions, that plan financial policies with an eye to their own best interest and feel little obligation to any particular government or people, are indeed global institutions. To advocates of "one world," the multinationals are the entering wedge of a new world order, since they will have to be regulated somehow and the only regulation that can control them adequately is a supranational one. Thus they will force a stronger world order. Nationalists take a different line. They believe the home government *and* the host government should ·control these corporations. The home government can lay down the law for its corporations' conduct, and the host government can keep the multinationals out, or nationalize them when that seems the best course. This is the simplest solution, but it is a solution that sacrifices many economic advantages, especially for a host society that is eager for development.

Some voices have been raised calling for the United Nations to become involved in the solution of the problem. One suggestion is the establishment of a universal "companies law" which a world agency would administer and under which cases would come before the International Court of Justice. Such a scheme would be a radical break with the past. It could be adopted only after careful study and long negotiation. It would undoubtedly tend to unify the world economy and could be so structured as to give the developing countries a more powerful position vis-à-vis the developed countries.[21]

Until the seventies, most observers and many U.N. agencies divided the nations of the world into two groups: the developed and the developing. This simplistic conception was shattered in 1973 by the embargo on oil from the Middle East. The demonstration that fossil fuels could be withheld from the world market, thus disrupting the economies of the industrialized countries and drastically reducing the supply of fertilizers used by the agricultural countries, was a severe shock to both groups. Even when the embargo was lifted, the staggering increase in prices set by the OPEC cartel left the rest of the world in economic disarray and deeply worried about the future. The problem of equitable access to scarce natural resources was raised in dramatic terms.

Oil, however, is not the only natural resource that is in short supply and for which substitutes may be required in a few decades. Industrial metals are especially worrisome. Accurate projections of the years of availability are impossible because the rate of acceleration in use and the rate of discovery of new reserves are both unknown. There is hope that mining the seabed will ease concern for supplies of maganese, copper, nickel and cobalt. There is not equal optimism, however, about supplies of tin, zinc, and aluminum. There is a real possibility that tin and zinc will become prohibitively costly early in the next century if a thorough system of recycling these metals is not set up in all industrialized countries.

Shortages of oil and metals not only forecast higher prices but, if cartels press their advantage, may give rise to wars. Veiled military threats were made during the oil embargo. If moves were ever made by Japan, the Common Market nations, or the United States against the Middle East, intervention by the Soviet Union would be almost certain. The necessity of dealing with this time bomb effectively is clear. World consideration of how to meet the challenge effectively is urgent. What needs to be done is so incompatible with national sovereignty that it certainly will not be done quickly. Were the United Nations to undertake its consideration now, there might well be resignations of powerful member states that would lead to that body's disintegration. A firmer world order must be established through success of other initiatives before this problem can be attacked.

The efforts of the United Nations to deal with other pressing global problems in addition to peace and security flow from the same basic orientation as that expressed in enlightened patriotism: concern for humanity. The pioneer nations and the chief world institutions have attitudes that are compatible and reinforcing. This is hopeful and reassuring. It makes it likely that strong efforts will be made to cure the U.N.'s bureaucratic deficiencies and to strengthen the commitment of its members. If the United Nations begins not only to show initiative in facing world problems but progress in mastering them, confidence in the system will mount and the outlook for world order will brighten.

7

Regional Intergovernmental Organizations

The speed and popularity of air travel after World War II gave rise to wider and more frequent connections between peoples of different nations. Out of these connections the tentative process of social growth produced an expanded set of international organizations. Perhaps the most powerful ones, though not the most numerous, were the intergovernmental organizations. In the twenty-two years between the 1952 edition and the 1974–75 edition of the *Yearbook of International Organizations*, the number of them unconnected with the United Nations system grew from 101 to 283. Of these, the regional organizations have been particularly relevant to the question of world order, since they lie between the nation and the U.N. system.

We may recognize roughly five kinds of regional organizations: the mutual security ones, like NATO; those formed to further the trading interest of the members, like the Latin American Free Trade Area; those based on cultural solidarity, like the Nordic Council; those having merely a consultative function, like the Asian and Pacific Council; and the purely technical ones, like the Danube Commission and the Customs Cooperation Council.

Statesmen and scholars concerned about world peace have

114 Quest for World Order

mixed feelings about regional organizations. For the most part they see the consultative ones and the purely technical ones as contributing to world order, as relieving the United Nations of tasks that can be handled effectively on a regional basis. These organizations weaken somewhat the autonomy of the nation and give experience in fruitful cooperation. Other types of intergovernmental organizations may be similarly conducive to peace, but they are not always so. Thus, a seemingly innocuous cultural organization like the Islamic Conference may become politicized in relation to a dispute like that between the Arab states and Israel.

When it is a question of market organizations, the danger that bitter rivalries may develop is great. The European Economic Community and the Council of Mutual Economic Assistance (formerly called COMECON, for Communist Economy) have so far struggled peacefully for a greater share of world trade, but a worldwide depression might lead to forms of cutthroat competition that would start a disastrous downward spiral culminating in violent reprisals.

Most threatening to world peace are, of course, the regional mutual security organizations. These are founded for the purpose of collective defense, but the definition of an aggressive act is so vague and uncertain that what one party sees as simply a new element of defense the other party sees as unjustifiable aggression. The sort of ambiguities that arise are well illustrated by the Cuban missile crisis of 1962. Cuba, recently turned Communist under Castro, feared attack by the United States and started to emplace medium-range missiles supplied by the Soviet Union. The United States, a member of NATO, interpreted this as a hostile act which extended the reach of the Warsaw Pact Organization into the Western hemisphere. The United States threatened to use military force to destroy the sites if the missiles were not removed; the Soviet Union insisted on Cuba's right to peaceful self-defense. The world teetered on the edge of war involving the two most powerful mutual security organizations.

The question whether mutual security blocs are less likely than nations to avoid the scourge of war is moot. Decisions are perhaps less erratic because coalitions make them, but the decision for war, when made, is more catastrophic. George Orwell's prescient novel *1984* painted a grim picture of a world dominated by three great blocs that were constantly at war—the two weaker at any time opposing the strongest, with a change in the alliance when relative power shifted.[1] It is clear that the world cannot be entrusted to the sole care of regional bodies. Some modus vivendi must be found to keep them from destroying one another.

Ernest B. Haas, one of the most eminent students of regionalism, gives hope that the United Nations will become the means.

> Uneasy balancing among blocs is the operative law of the United Nations life in our era. The United Nations functions, not despite alliances outside its scope, but *because* of their presence and countervailing claims. . . . Interregional adjustment through multilateral diplomacy and not the test of the Charter is now the basis of United Nations action. . . . Even if world law and order are not advanced through this *de facto* reconciliation, nevertheless a modicum of stability may be introduced. This in turn may give rise to expectations of peaceful coexistence, making recourse to the military clauses of contemporary alliances unlikely.[2]

Haas's terms "uneasy balancing" and a "modicum of stability" are well chosen. The present controls over mutual security organizations are, to mix metaphors, weak reeds yielding slender hopes.

The danger from regional security organizations is enhanced by the ambiguities in the provision of the U.N. Charter relating to them. In general, the Security Council is given jurisdiction over threats to peace and security. Article 51, however, makes a specific exception that allows a regional body to take collective security measures in response to an armed attack on one of its members. That body must immediately report such measures to the Security Council, and, by Article 53, all subsequent enforcement actions must be approved by the Council. Moreover, by Article 54 the Security Council must be informed in advance of all activities in contemplation for maintenance of peace and security. It is unclear whether the imposition of economic sanctions on a non-member by a regional group comes under Articles 53 and 54.

This ambiguity might lead to dangerous situations. Suppose, for instance, that NATO, on complaints by Norway, Iceland, Canada, and the United States of the transgressions of the Soviet fishing fleet, imposed economic sanctions on the Soviet Union. A majority of the Security Council might regard this as a collective security measure calling for transfer of jurisdiction to the Security Council. Britain, a permanent member of the Council, might then veto the transfer in the belief that the United Nations would not take vigorous action. The world would be exposed to the risk of hostilities between the Soviet Union and NATO.

Looking back, it seems as if the 1945–75 period in international affairs had two distinct phases of roughly equal length. Up to 1961, international relations exemplified what has been called a tight bipolar system. The United States headed the Western, capitalist bloc; the Soviet Union the Eastern, Communist bloc. As the only two nations with large stocks of nuclear weapons, they were the most powerful states in the world. NATO and the Warsaw Pact Organization became the protagonists in the Cold War. The membership of other intergovernmental organizations tended to reflect the cleavage thus produced.

Several commentators have seen the second postwar phase as one of declining bipolar rigidity. They attribute this to two influential changes. One was the multiplication of political actors on the world stage. The breakup of the British, French,

Dutch, Belgian, and Portugese overseas empires has spawned numerous independent states, twenty-six of which joined the United Nations in the years 1960–62. These began to have political influence, contributed to the complexity of international relations, and gave a wider field of political maneuver. At almost the same time the second change occurred. The two superpowers found it wise to moderate the Cold War. The Soviet Union became worried about the growing strength and hostile attitude of Communist China, and the United States became heavily involved in Vietnam. Thus the controls that had been exerted through the Warsaw Pact and NATO, constraining and channeling the interactions among nations, were somewhat relaxed. The potentials of the networks of communication and transportation gradually became more fully realized. Nations increased their trade across the Iron Curtain and the nations of Asia showed surprising fluctuations in their mutual attachments. The tentative process became more spirited.

One way of putting the matter would be to say that with greater freedom of maneuver there was more randomness of relationships. Old uniformities were gone. Unintended consequences were more frequent because nations were acting in a more complex and puzzling world. It was harder to anticipate how others would act.

This kind of world, which perhaps came to its peak of unpredictability with the entrance of the Peoples Republic of China into the United Nations, the withdrawal of the United States from Indochina, and the dramatic political shifts in Portugal and Spain, is seen by some political analysts as weakening the mutual security organizations and thus reducing the threat of war. They see entropy in the international system as leveling old power differentials and ushering in a new and more humane world order. In my view, this loosening up of the system may well be what is needed to stimulate the development of a different pattern of relations, but it is not the first step toward realizing a new world order. So far, it merely marks a slackening of ties and an increase of confusion.

There is, however, hope for reducing the risk deriving from hostile mutual security organizations in another possiblity, one unintended by anyone. This is that the process known as crisscrossing might be moving the world inconspicuously toward world order. Crisscrossing occurs whenever two units in any field of social interaction find themselves allies on one issue but opponents on another. The concept is more easily illustrated by considering four units involved in two different cleavages. Suppose that units A and B oppose units C and D on one issue, but, on another issue, A and C are partners against B and D. A simple example would be four business enterprises whose owners line up two against two on a street-widening proposal and are again two against two in a campaign for mayor, but this time with changed partners.

The general theory is that the more crisscrossing of this kind there is in any area of interaction, the less the danger of serious conflict among the participants. In 1923, the distinguished American sociologist, Edward Alsworth Ross, expounded this theory with his usual clarity.

> Every species of conflict interferes with every other species in society at the same time, save only when their lines of cleavage coincide; in which case they reinforce one another.[3]
>
> These various oppositions in society are like different wave series set up on opposite sides of a lake, which neutralize each other if the crests of one meet the troughs of another, but which reinforce each other if crest meets crest while trough meets trough.[4]
>
> A society, therefore, which is riven by a dozen oppositions along lines running in every direction, may actually be in less danger of being torn with violence or falling to pieces than one split along just one line. Each new cleavage contributes to narrow crossclefts, so that

one might say that society *is sewn together* by its inner
conflicts. It is not such a paradox after all if one re-
members that every species of collective strife tends to
knit together with a sense of fellowship the contenders
on either side.[5]

A contemporary sociologist applies this insight to the United
States.

American society is simply riddled with cleavages. The
remarkable phenomenon is the extent to which the various differences "cancel out"—are noncumulative in
their incidence. There is much realistic sociological
meaning in *e pluribus unum*.[6]

Crisscrossing in this sense is rare in relations among nations.
The one most commented on consists of a North-South cleavage in the U.N. General Assembly between developed and
developing countries that crosscuts the East-West ideological
cleavage. The Soviet bloc and the Western bloc have been
opposed to each other on many issues for three decades, but
since 1960 the North-South cleavage over the extent of aid that
the United Nations should give to developing countries has
found them in the same (North) camp. Similarly, capitalist and
Communist countries came together in the South camp. The
demand of the developing countries at the United Nations for
a new economic order (discussed in chapter 6) has deepened
the North-South cleavage. As a result, nations that have seen
eye to eye ideologically are experiencing some strain in their
relations: France and the Ivory Coast, for example; and the
Soviet Union and Sudan. Such strains show that cross pressures exerted by crisscrossing could ultimately mitigate
capitalist-Communist conflicts.

Crosscutting cleavages at the international level are rare
because of the complexity of the situation which must occur.
There must be two conflicts, each of them pitting groups of
nations against each other, with some nations active partners in

one struggle but opponents in the other. This pattern occurs frequently in the local community, but it does not happen often when the participants are national governments interacting in the world arena. As a matter of fact, the East-West, North-South crosscutting discussed above does not exemplify perfectly the full pattern because there is no official organization of the North camp to match the original Committee of Seventy-seven of the developing nations (since expanded to a larger organization).

Contributing to the rarity of crisscrossing is the unwillingness of statesmen to have their nation get into a situation where the government is cross-pressured by standing with fellow nations on one issue and rejecting their position on another issue. This may, in fact, be a rational course and one which the national constituency applauds, but the government that follows it is likely to be denigrated as a fair-weather friend who is inconsistent in foreign policy. This situation is particularly difficult when one of the commitments is to a mutual security organization. It would be very hard for Norway, for example, to take a stand in the United Nations supporting the efforts of the developing countries to control the activities of multinational corporations if all the other members of NATO were opposed to such control.

Interesting as is the theory that crosscutting conflicts "sew together" a society, and much as it may be validated within nations, there is little evidence that it occurs often enough at the international level to strengthen world order materially. There is, however, a less complex situation which is also less effective in each instance than crisscrossing, but which occurs frequently enough to be worth study.

The phenomenon I refer to is bridging. This occurs when, in addition to two organizations struggling across a cleavage, there is a third organization among whose members are nations from both sides of the cleavage. This third organization, then, forms a bridge between the other two. For example, the NATO nations and the Warsaw Pact nations have been engaged in ideological struggle since 1948; but the North East

Atlantic Fisheries Commission, an IGO, is somewhat of a bridge between them because the Soviet Union and Poland are members, along with Belgium, Denmark, France, West Germany, Iceland, the Netherlands, Norway, and Britain. Such a bridging organization will not have as much influence in softening the struggle between the two mutual security organizations as it would if the fisheries commission had as an opponent a meat producers organization that also had members in both camps. The latter situation would exemplify crisscrossing and would produce stronger cooperation of the members of the two occupational groups across the ideological cleavage.

Even bridging, however, involves some cross-pressure and, in cases of severe conflict among IGOs, it rarely occurs. Thus, the long struggle between the League of Arab States and Israel has not been bridged at all by governmental organizations other than those of the United Nations system. A similar strong cleavage with few bridges exists between the black sub-Saharan African states and the white-governed nations of Rhodesia and South Africa.

Though bridging is not so powerful a force as crisscrossing, I decided to study the trends in it between 1964 and 1974 through data on intergovernmental organizations in the *Yearbook of International Organizations*. Like crisscrossing, bridging does not occur from any peaceful intention on the part of nations. They join bridging organizations for the same reason that they join other intergovernmental organizations: to achieve national goals. Since there were cleavages among the seven mutual security organizations existing from 1964 and 1974, I investigated the frequency of bridging across those cleavages. In doing so I imposed certain limitations on my use of the data in the appropriate editions of the *Yearbook of International Organizations*. These limitations are discussed in appendix C.

Imposing limitations on the task was not the only problem in planning the research. Another was how to deal with the fact that the mutual security organizations had overlapping memberships. Obviously one could not regard the North Atlantic Treaty Organization and the Organization of American States as having a cleavage between them, even though they had but one common member—the United States. The only one of the seven organizations that had no overlaps with the other six was the Warsaw Pact Organization. The North Atlantic Treaty Organization and the South East Asia Treaty Organization had the most overlaps in membership: both of them with the Central Treaty Organization, the Organization of American States, and each other. The only other case of overlap involved the Organization of African Unity and the League of Arab States.[7] Despite these overlaps, clear cleavages existed among the memberships of the seven organizations as follows:

Warsaw Pact vs. NATO   NATO vs. League of
Warsaw Pact vs. SEATO   Arab States
Warsaw Pact vs. CENTO   NATO vs. OAU
Warsaw Pact vs. OAS   SEATO vs. League of
Warsaw Pact vs.   Arab States
    League of Arab States   SEATO vs. OAU
Warsaw Pact vs. OAU   CENTO vs. League of
OAS vs. League of Arab   Arab States
    States   CENTO vs. OAU
OAS vs. OAU   CENTO vs. OAS

It is interesting to look at the superpowers in the perspective of these cleavages. The Soviet Union is a member of one mutual security organization (the Warsaw Pact Organization, with six other members) that has no overlaps and faces six cleavages. The United States was, in 1974, a member of three security organizations (NATO, SEATO, and OAS) that overlapped with each other and had forty-two other nation members. All three of these organizations experience cleavages with the Warsaw Pact Organization, the Arab League, and the OAU. From this evidence, however, one cannot draw the conclusion that either the United States or the Soviet Union is the more secure. Mutual security organizations cut both ways.

They are assets because others are bound to aid you and liabilities because you are bound to aid them.

In my study of bridging, I set out to determine its increase or decrease over time and to find some way to compare its relative significance to that of countervailing trends. The first of these tasks was straightforward. I looked at all the intergovernmental organizations that met my criteria in the 1964 and 1974 *Yearbooks* to find the ones that included members from both sides of any mutual security cleavage. There were twenty-one such organizations in 1964 and thirty in 1974. This is a 52.4 percent increase in ten years, a crude measure because it does not take account of the fact that a single organization may function as several bridges. An organization, for instance, three of whose members are the United States, the Soviet Union, and Saudi Arabia, would by that very fact be bridging the cleavages between NATO and the Warsaw Pact Organization, NATO and the Arab League, and the Warsaw Pact Organization and the Arab League. Such an organization is more effective in contributing to global integration than a three-nation organization forming only one bridge. It is worthwhile, therefore, to count the number of bridges in 1964 and 1974. They turn out to be, 107 and 147, respectively. This produces a growth rate of 37.4 percent. But even this does not reflect the number of members of mutual security organizations on the bridges. (A bridging organization may, of course, contain nations that are not members of security organizations.) The 1964 number of members of mutual security organizations on bridges was 366; the 1974 number, 552. This is an increase of 50.8 percent.

At first glance these figures seem encouraging, showing increased contacts of members of mutual security organizations across cleavages. There are more IGOs containing bridges in 1974 than in 1964, more bridges are created by these organizations, and more members of mutual security organizations are participating in the bridges. One could draw the conclusion that forces are at work which favor the growth of world order.

There is another side to the picture, however. While bridging through IGOs was increasing, nonbridging by IGOs was also increasing, and at a faster rate. This can be shown in several ways. While nine additional bridging organizations were added between 1964 and 1974, eighteen nonbridging IGOs were also added. While the number of participations in bridging IGOs by members of security organizations was growing by 50.8 percent, the number of such participations in nonbridging IGOs increased by 165.2 percent.

The meaning of these data is clear: two processes are going on side by side. One is the bridging of cleavages; the other is the reinforcement of the clusters of nations identified by mutual security organizations. Both of these tendencies are increasing rapidly, but the reinforcement is occurring at a faster pace than the bridging. Essentially what is happening is that the nations are knitting themselves together worldwide, but in such a manner as to protect their basic security groupings. It is a process that is very similar to what goes on within a nation—the metropolises become more closely connected with each other, but at the same time each metropolitan area becomes a denser web of relations within itself. Just as we speak of the nation as becoming organized by these twin developments, so we can consider the world as becoming organized by the twin developments that our figures delineate.

This picture closely parallels what John Higham has seen as a possibility for ethnic relations in the United States. Speaking of a way to effect dual commitment to a common national culture and the preservation of distinct ethnic cultures, he has said:

> In principle this dual commitment might be met by distinguishing between boundaries and nuclei. No ethnic group under these terms can have the support of the general community in strengthening its bound-

aries. All boundaries are understood to be permeable. Ethnic nuclei, on the other hand, are respected as enduring centers of social action. If self-preservation requires, they may claim exemption from certain universal rules, as the Amish now do from the school laws in some states. Both integration and ethnic cohesion are recognized as worthy goals, which different individuals will accept in different degrees. Ethnicity varies enormously in intensity from one person to another. It will have some meaning for the great majority of Americans, but total meaning for relatively few. Only minorities of minorities, so to speak, will find in ethnic identity an exclusive loyalty.[8]

Higham's suggested model is what all the candidates for the presidency of the United States were trying, ineffectively, to describe in their 1976 campaigns. President Carter almost ruined his chances by saying that he would not tamper with the "ethnic purity" of American neighborhoods. What he meant was that he would not try to do away with ethnic nuclei. He did not mean to imply that he would encourage borders.

In earlier chapters we have encountered enlightened patriotism, a way of harmonizing national and global commitment. With Higham's concept of nuclei, we see how regional groups can maintain their special interests and still reject the exclusiveness that borders represent. Indeed, concurrent developments in three directions are compatible—in enlightened patriotism, regional nuclei, and world order. This is not to say that such a happy state of affairs is in the cards. The reinforcing of regional groupings might begin to produce borders and thus handicap both enlightened patriotism and world order. As the next chapter will show, however, such a trend is unlikely because of the rapid growth of the web of international nongovernmental relations. Bridging through IGOs may not increase rapidly, but there is no present prospect that it will lose its conciliating influence.

8

The Web of International Nongovernmental Relations

The last chapter identified a process, the bridging of cleavages between nations by intergovernmental organizations, that might facilitate the growth of world order. This chapter will shift the focus to the web of nongovernmental relations. Three facets of these relations will be probed: international nongovernmental organizations, other forms of transnational experience, and the convergence of cultural values.

The research reported in chapter 3 has already shown that INGO participation is a powerful predictor of national support for world order. There is little need, therefore, to go into an extensive discussion of these organizations. The prime source of general information about them is published biennially by the International Union of Associations. In the 1974–75 edition of its *Yearbook of International Organizations*, there were 2,574 INGOs on which information was given. These are clustered into the following categories: bibliography, documentation, press; religion, ethics; social sciences; humanistic studies; international relations; politics; law, administration; social welfare; professions, employers; trade unions; economics, finance; commerce, industry; agriculture; transportation, trade; technology; science; health, medicine; education, youth; arts, literature, radio, cinema, TV; sports, recreation; Common Market business and professional organizations; and European Free Trade Association (EFTA) business and professional organizations. The largest category is health, medicine with 288 entries. In this field almost every specialty has a worldwide organization. The category of commerce, industry is a close second. The significance of the Common Market (European Economic Community) to its members is demonstrated by the existence of 246 non-governmental organizations linking nationals of the constituent nations, making that category the third largest. Generally speaking, the regional INGOs like those fostered by the Common Market, have conferences yearly, but most worldwide organizations gather in large congresses less frequently— every third or fourth year. In the interim there are usually annual meetings of their executive committees. Many INGOs foster research and other projects appropriate to the functions in life of their members.

INGO participation is increasing rapidly. In the 1964–65 *Yearbook of International Organizations*, 1,718 INGOs were listed. Ten years later the number was 2,574. This is a yearly rate of increase of 4.3 percent. The rate is lower than that cited in *Peace on the March*, which showed an increase of 9.4 percent a year for the six years between 1956–57 and 1962–63.[1] It was in those years, however, that INGOs focussing on labor and business relations were being founded within the European Economic Community, accounting for almost one-fifth of the total growth in INGOs. Coupling the data from the two periods yields a growth over the eighteen-year period between 1956–57 and 1974–75 from 958 to 2,574, or a yearly increase of 7.3 percent. This growth shows that a rapidly increasing number of people around the world are having the opportunity to meet and work with citizens of other nations. My own experience confirms the presumption from the evidence in chapter 3: that more of these participants are learning to trust than to distrust one another.[2]

One hopeful aspect of the Middle Eastern situation, ac-

cording to a Scandinavian investigator, is that despite the lack of intergovernmental bridges between the Arab League and Israel, citizens of Israel and citizens of the surrounding Arab countries have common memberships in many INGOs which could serve as informal channels for negotiations. He also points out that Cyprus, Romania, and India have many ties with both sides of the Mideast conflict.[3]

A development that is hopeful because it indicates growing equality in the transnational network is the declining dominance of European nations in the location of INGO headquarters. Whereas 83.2 percent of the headquarters listed in the 1962–63 *Yearbook of International Organizations* were in Europe, by 1974–75 the corresponding figure was 79.2 percent.

We have regarded INGO participation as one of the causes of national support for world order because the two were proven well correlated by empirical research. The other kinds of transnational participation discussed in *Peace on the March* were not made variables in the study of national support for world order because reliable data on them were not available for enough countries. Several of them will, however, be briefly discussed here as strengthening the web of relations among nations. I shall take up first the visiting of relatives and friends abroad.

Because the visitors undertake the trip and the hosts put themselves out to receive the visitors, it is assumed that both visitors and hosts expect the visit to be rewarding. Since a visit is almost always to a home, the host couple usually wants to introduce their guests to neighbors and friends. Thus the visitors form acquaintances in a broader circle. The meeting of the two nationalities takes place under friendly auspices and is likely to be a pleasant experience, because both the foreign and the local guests want to make a good impression. Then, too, hosts like to show guests the more attractive aspects of the community in which they live. In short, the foreign guests get a positive feeling toward both the people and the place and are likely to go home with a sense of warmth toward the nation as a whole. Those whom they have met tend to reciprocate that feeling toward them and their country.

There is no way to estimate with any accuracy the worldwide number of visits to relatives and friends abroad. My previous study did find, however, an estimated yearly increase of 11 percent in passengers crossing the Atlantic from New York by air and sea for this purpose during the period 1956–57 to 1963–64. This was probably due to increasing affluence. If so, it would indicate a general growth in travel for this purpose, since most countries were then enjoying an upward economic trend. More recent economic stringencies may have retarded this growth. Another limiting influence may be the increasing lapse of time since the great migration to the Western Hemisphere from Europe, beginning in the mid-nineteenth century and continuing to World War I. This growing interval is decreasing the number of families, in both the Old World and the New, that have close relatives in the opposite hemisphere. Though transnational visits are positive in their effect and therefore facilitative of attempts to strengthen world order, it is uncertain what their trend will be.

Another widespread form of transnational participation is study abroad for undergraduate or graduate work. The UNESCO Statistical Yearbook for 1971 reveals that (in that year) 2 percent of all college and university students around the globe were in foreign countries —528,744 of them. This total had risen from 266,000 in 1962, a rate of yearly increase of 11.4 percent. The largest movement is from developing to developed countries. These students undoubtedly have been seeking kinds of training they could not obtain so well at home. More than 140,126 were studying in the United States. This was 26.5 percent of all students abroad. France had the next largest number—36,500. The continent of origin of the largest proportion—38.9 percent—was Asia, the leading countries being Taiwan and Jordan. With the expansion of colleges and universities in developing countries, it is expected that the curve of increase in those going abroad will flatten out.

Much research has been conducted to evaluate study abroad. Some of the topics investigated have been the student's problems of adjustment, his academic achievement, his absorption of the culture of the host nation, and his attitude toward the native students. More relevant to the effect on accommodation among nations is the attitude toward host nationals and their government at the time of departure for home. In developing friendly attitudes toward the host nation, however, the foreign students may have picked up its animosities toward third nations. Nigerian students in the United States, for instance, may have acquired hostile attitudes toward the Soviet Union. To quote my previous study:

> The effect on him [the foreign student] is not positive unless he sees his own experience with the host country as one that he might enjoy with the people of many nations. Only if the particular experience is thus generalized is he likely to influence his own policymakers toward international accomodation when he returns home.[4]

The evidence from the twenty-one studies examined on the effects (both on the foreign and the host students) is mixed, but on balance seems slightly positive. One broad generalization seems supported by these studies: that friendly relations while abroad and a positive effect in later life occur more often when the country of origin and the country of study are on a similar level of development. The most positive effects reported were in investigations of Swedish students in the United States and American students in France. Franklin Scott interviewed fifty Swedish individuals, nineteen of whom had been students abroad nineteen to thirty-one years earlier and thirty-one of whom had been abroad up to eight years earlier. He found that:

> One of the returnees is an officer in a movement for world union. Some hold positions at various levels in

the United Nations. One might be called a technological statesman on a high international plane. These are all from the prewar group (World War II) while among the postwar group at least eight of the subjects were attracted to further international study or activity. In at least three of the latter cases the interest was born in American colleges and represents deflection from previous plans.

Very few of the subjects escaped some significant extensions of mental horizons. . . . In the majority of instances what happens is that mind and heart expand to encompass more than before without destroying loyalty to country or love of native heath.[5]

C. Robert Pace investigated the effects on 150 American students of a junior year in France. He compared them with a control group of matched individuals who had not gone abroad. To quote my summary:[6]

He found that on nine kinds of activities related to interest in other countries, the United Nations, and foreign policy, 30 percent of the controls engaged in five or more activities as contrasted with 47 percent of the participants. When queried on nine policies connected with exchange of persons, technical assistance, international free trade, and the like, 77 percent of the participants versus 59 percent of the controls favored eight or nine of these policies. Pace checked carefully the possibility that these differences resulted mainly from the greater language facility of the participants. He found that this was not so. Within the participant group, language facility was not linked to the degree of accomodative orientation. Another significant finding was that foreign travel, independent of foreign study, had very little effect either on the participants or the controls. Pace summarizes his finding as follows: "Within the scope of the present inquiry . . . the data gathered and analyzed lead one to conclude that there is an impact which is both strong and pervasive. It goes far beyond the impact of travel for personal pleasure."[7]

Reassuring as these studies are, they pertain to linkages of countries at the same level of development. They give no insight into study abroad when countries involved are at different levels.

A less positive picture emerges when students from developing nations are studying in developed nations. There seem to be two related reasons for this. One is that there is often lack of understanding, mistrust, and even hostility in the country of origin; the other is a feeling of superiority in the country of study. This is particularly well illustrated in a study by Beals and Humphrey of Mexican students in the United States. They found that the students were aware, before they left home, of charges of imperialism against the United States. During their stay they felt some discrimination by Americans. Furthermore, they were critical of American family life, felt the United States was too materialistic, and that it was deficient in aesthetic appreciation. However, they appreciated the high quality of the training they received and liked the greater freedom of women and the emphasis on individuality, which surprised them. When they returned to Mexico, they kept alive their links to the United States and influenced Mexican organizations to participate in international meetings. Thus, they encouraged accommodation on the instrumental level but did not favor national convergence on the level of values.[8]

There was some of the same critical orientation revealed in an inquiry on students from India in the United States by Lambert and Bressler.[9] The students were exposed, before leaving home, to criticism of the materialism and the militarism of the United States and were expected to keep aloof from such influences during their residence. When they arrived, they found condescension in the attitudes of

American students. Related to this, Lambert and Bressler emphasize "sensitive areas."[10] In my own words:

> They learned that many Americans think that India is inferior, is undesirable to live in because its people have objectionable traits, has an inhumane social struc- ture, and is a threat to the world because of its popula- tion growth. The Indian develops defense mechanisms against these criticisms but the situation is quite tense. Though the Indians like to travel through the United States, admire much that they see, and believe that the training they are receiving will be important for them and for India, the situation does not seem likely to fos- ter accommodative attitudes.[11]

A complementary study by John and Ruth Hill Useem of 110 Indian students who had been educated in Britain and the United States shows the situation at a later stage.[12] In my words:

> . . . they found that one-third of their respondents felt that their experience had broadened their social hori- zons. The authors note three themes running through the interviews with this third. The first is a realization of the unity of mankind. A typical quotation illustrates this: "I came to know that not only in India but everywhere there is trouble. I also came to see that we are all one human family—this is what I saw." A second theme is that earlier criticism of the values and norms of the Western world turned to toleration, even ap- preciation: "Going to another country enabled me to get behind all ideologies and to see that every people have ideals." Finally, the respondents confessed to great- er openness toward others and their ideas: "I realized that there was something vaster, something bigger; you feel humble for knowledge and you gain respect for the opinion of others. I thought of India only before, now I think of the whole world."[13]

The Beals and Humphrey and the Lambert and Bressler studies both show a mixed result. Though the returnees did not love the United States, they acknowledged that they had received practical benefits from their study abroad and they felt some broadening of their horizons. Perhaps they became more enlightened patriots.

There is very little research on the effects that foreign students have on the students of the host society with whom they come in contact. The latter, however, are experiencing transnational participation too. One illuminating study was done at Indiana University.[14] I quote from my own account:

> In the fall of 1963 all foreign students at that institution were sent a questionnaire. Seventy percent responded. One of the items asked them to name their close American friends. Careful interviews were then carried out, with two sets of American students, in the Graduate Residence Center in which 277 of the foreign students lived. The first set consisted of 148 American students named as close friends; the second set consisted of 330 not named as close friends. This gave the opportunity to compare the effects òn Americans who were experiencing different degrees of transnational participation.[15]

The comparison, the details of which I shall not show here, gives strong evidence that those who were named as close friends had more often changed their future plans for travel, courses and languages, vocations, and the Peace Corps than had the students not named as close friends. This seems to show that aspects of life that are related to foreign students become more salient to their intimate friends than to others. This is, perhaps, for the American students the first step in concern for humanity in general.

Closely related to study abroad is residence abroad of college and university professors for teaching or research. Sources of data are so scant that I hesitate to give an estimate of the yearly number abroad or the rate of increase. •The data on airline travel from New York for U.S. citizens going abroad and citizens of foreign countries returning home yield a better clue to the rate of increase than to the numbers involved. Two studies were made, seven years apart, in 1956–57 and 1963–64. They showed, for both American and foreign professors crossing the Atlantic for stays of more than six months, a yearly increase of some 15 percent.[16] This is probably too high a rate for the world as a whole, since the economic growth of the United States and West European countries during those years was more rapid than for the rest of the world. Ten percent might be nearer the mark. Worldwide, it appears (from several clues that I shall not go into) that the total number of professionals residing abroad for teaching or research by 1975 could hardly have been less than 70,000.

The best study of the effects of teaching and research abroad is one by the United States Department of State evaluating the Fulbright program.[17] A sample of 958 professors furnished the information. More than half had engaged in collaborative research with foreign professors or graduate students; 85 percent had presented papers to foreign professional bodies; and a similar proportion maintained relations with scholars of the host country after their return. Half arranged reciprocal visits of foreign colleagues to the United States. One indication of their continued interest in the host country was that 80 percent had entertained persons in their homes who had been referred to them by friends abroad. It seems clear that a year of teaching or research initiates a lasting tie. This conclusion is confirmed by a smaller study carried out at the University of Massachusetts.[18]

The conclusion that teaching and research abroad contribute to better relations between nations has one specific exception: animosity is aroused by social scientists who conduct research on controversial matters in foreign countries. The resentment of Chilean scholars to plans for an American-supported study of counterinsurgency in Chile, a resentment that forced the abandonment in 1965 of Project Camelot, is a striking case in point. This exception needs to be put in perspective, however. For every scholar who has offended the country in which he has done research, there are scores who have not done so, and dozens whose work has been appreciated.

The evidence examined shows, in general, that study abroad and teaching and research abroad work toward accommodation among nations and hence world order. With the exception noted in the last paragraph, the residence abroad of professors seems to have more positive effects than the residence abroad of students—both on the visitors and those with whom they come in contact. It is almost certain that faculty experience has more influence on public opinion than student experience. Maturity and status give their views on international matters more weight and probably earn wider notice. One should not forget, however, that college students who have been abroad may have potential influence in their later careers. Since the individuals who have studied abroad will be increasing in all countries for the next few decades, the impact of the friendships they have made may have a positive effect.

A significant but less common form of transnational experience is working abroad to help a developing country meet its problems. There are three main types: voluntary service either in a summer camp or a peace corps; bilateral technical assistance in which a government sends specialists among its nationals to render needed services; and multilateral technical assistance in which the United Nations or one of its specialized agencies recruits and sends experts for the same purpose.

The first organized voluntary work on behalf of a sister nation seems to have occurred after World War I, when youth from Switzerland and Germany joined their peers in France to help clear the rubble from war-devastated Verdun. Soon thereafter summer work camps were organized in several countries by Service Civil International. Following World War II, the increase in such camps was rapid. Religious bodies sponsored many of them. UNESCO established the Coordinating Committee for International Voluntary Work Camps in 1948. This committee has been unable to keep track of all the camps that have been set up around the world or to determine what the proportion of foreigners to natives is. It has been generally assumed that the camps have produced greater understanding between peoples.

To my knowledge, only one thorough evaluative study has been carried out.[19] Fourteen groups of American youth went to West Africa in "Operation Crossroads." The members of three groups who worked in Nigeria, Ghana, and Guinea were interviewed about their experience. Those who volunteered for this work were, of course, already humanely motivated. The evidence from the study shows that, although they were occasionally impatient of the Africans' inability to slough off traditional practices quickly, they came to respect them. The original accomodative attitude of the Americans was maintained.

It is perhaps more illuminating to ask what the effects were on the natives. Here the evidence is strongly positive. The Africans admired the strangers for coming so far, with no renumeration, to help another country and were much impressed by the willingness of college students, and particularly girls, to work enthusiastically at hard, manual jobs. Although the Africans realized that these were not wholly typical Americans, the author of the study concludes that the image of the United States as a nation was much improved.

Reports such as these no doubt inspired President Kennedy to inaugurate the United States Peace Corps in 1961. The example of the United States has been followed by some fifteen other nations. Though such corps have been established by governments, the relations of the participants to the native peoples are of a person-to-person sort rather than government-to-government. It is estimated that there were some 20,000 peace corps participants abroad from all countries by 1965 and that the number has remained steady since.

The effects of work in a peace corps are very difficult to summarize. When I wrote *Peace on the March*, I relied heavily on three studies that had been made before 1967 on volunteers in the United States corps: a study of 50 teachers in Ghana; one of 52 corpsmen and 343 natives in a community development program in Colombia; and one of a group of volunteers in the Peruvian Andes, including reactions to them by the native population. In my discussion, I made the point that it is not to be expected that Peace Corps volunteers will become much more positive in their feelings toward the nationals of the host country, because they start with a high level of idealism and anticipation. It was reassuring, therefore, to find from the studies that the volunteers came to identify with those with whom they were working and frequently kept in touch with them after their return home. The effects on the natives were strongly positive. In the Colombian study, for example, of 266 natives who had opinions one way or the other about the United States, 245 held positive opinions and of them 109 said their opinions had not been positive before the Peace Corps came.

Since that time, Brent Ashabranner's *A Moment in History*: *The First Ten Years of the Peace Corps* has been published.[20] It gives a thoughtful analysis of the whole effort, including both accomplishments and failures. A very clear finding is that the fine reputation of the Peace Corps in the first five years, when its trainees grew from 4,431 to 11,210, became tarnished by the Vietnam war. In several countries the Peace Corps came to be seen as a hypocritical gesture of a belligerent, imperialistic nation. Many college students in the United States shared this opinion. Some volunteers abroad joined in the criticism of U.S. policy. The Peace Corps administration was faced with the difficult dilemma of either supporting the volunteers and thus incurring the displeasure of some members of Congress, or calling home the critics and thus incurring the displeasure of the corps generally and of the countries in which the critics were working. Of sixty-four countries to which the Peace Corps had been sent, eight asked that the volunteers be withdrawn because of the host government's mounting hostility toward United States foreign policy. In two other cases no new requests were made for volunteers. A nation like Norway has had the advantage with its corps of having a foreign policy more acceptable to underdeveloped countries.

The success of the United States effort from the standpoint of the volunteers is attested by the fact that "94 percent of those who completed their service between the spring of 1963 and the fall of 1965 stated that, if they had it all to do over again and knowing all that they knew about the two years of service, they would still join the Peace Corps."[21] On the side of the native people, Mr. Ashabranner sums up:

> While the Peace Corps has often been seen in political terms by country leaders, this has not been true of the people with whom the volunteers have lived and worked. Feelings of nationalism and xenophobia, with surprisingly few exceptions, have not been a problem for volunteers in carrying out their daily work or overcoming the cultural and communicative problems that stand in the way of friendship. I believe that the bridges that have been built between people through the Peace Corps' having been in the country—even when the program has been broken off—may withstand the pressures of time and politics and be there for use at a future time.[22]

Until recently developing countries welcomed both bilateral and multilateral aid for development, but many of them are having second thoughts, particularly about bilateral aid. They fear that this is a form of neocolonialism and that they would be well advised to reject it and rely more on their own efforts. In view of this new attitude, it is doubtful whether humanitarian aid will be a growing source of world solidarity.

A form of transnational participation not discussed in *Peace on the March* is the cooperation of experts in studying global problems. This has been quite a recent development. In the past, few people have realized that the world, as distinct from nations, has unique problems, and fewer still have had a level of concern that induced transnational collaboration in their study. The fact of such collaboration was implied in discussing United Nations approaches to these problems in chapter 6, but the contribution to world solidarity that the *process* of this collaboration is likely to make was not taken up.

Since World War II there have been three striking examples of this process. The first is the series of Pugwash Conferences on Science and World Affairs. These have brought together scientists from both sides of the Cold War to discuss what they could do to help avoid a nuclear catastrophe. The first conference was held in Pugwash, Nova Scotia, in 1957. Some twenty-five more have been held in various places around the world. Although the proceedings are not made public, it is understood that such matters as the perfection of fail-safe procedures, the degree of provocation expressed through various ballistic and antiballistic missle systems, and methods of inspection for violation of disarmament agreements have been discussed. It has been reported that the repeated contacts of the participating scientists have given rise to transnational cooperation and have aided the disarmament negotiations of the United States and the Soviet Union. It seems generally agreed that the conferences have had little impact on public opinion in the countries whose scientists have been involved.

Another example of transnational collaboration on global problems is the work of the Club of Rome that was mentioned in chapter 1. The club is an informal group of 100 leaders from many countries, mostly Europeans, who were first brought together in 1968 by Alexander H. King, a

British scientist with broad international experience, and Aurelio Peccei, an Italian industrialist and economist. It has fostered studies aimed to help plan solutions to such world problems as hunger, overpopulation, scarcity of resources, pollution, and capital formation in developing countries. The distinctive approach of the Club of Rome is systems theory. Its early studies have been computer simulations of what will occur, given present knowledge of the inter-dependence of the basic variables. The first study by the club, *Limits to Growth*, stimulated a wide range of studies on this and other problems, and the club itself has brought out new studies looking toward action programs.

A less known collaboration of the same general kind is that being carried forward by the World Order Models Project. This effort, originated by a group of legal and social scientists in the United States, is concerned with the creation of a pre-ferred model for the future world. It has stimulated the forma-tion of half a dozen similar groups in other parts of the world. The first world meeting of the combined groups was held in New Delhi in 1968. Others have followed. Each group is work-ing out its own design, so that a process of world discussion may ensue on their completion. All designs are to represent the values of peace, human welfare, social justice, and ecologi-cal balance. Four volumes, each representing the design of one of the regional groups, have been completed.[23] Representing as it does a decentralized effort, the World Order Models Project promises to strengthen the cross-national ties of world-concerned scholars.

These beginnings are hopeful because they prefigure something that may be of great significance in furthering human solidarity: the growth among a wide spectrum of sci-entists and scholars of a sense of "one world." The formation of these networks is being facilitated by the numerous INGOs in many fields of knowledge. These networks will be composed not only of individual researchers, but of groups working together in universities and independent centers and insti-tutes. As more and more investigators become involved, links

will become stronger through newsletters, specialized journals, monograph series, and the like. The journal *Futures* is
already serving this function.

The prestige of scientists is such that a growing sense of
global solidarity among them and their colleagues will tend to
waken a similar sense among professionals outside universities
with whom they associate. The spread of this sentiment into
the well-educated stratum of national populations around the
world will be slow but, barring an intervening nuclear catastrophe, sure. The awareness that dedicated experts from
many countries are working together in teams to avert the
threat of global breakdown should arouse feelings of a common cause.

I have discussed six kinds of transnational participation—
membership in INGOs, visiting relatives and friends, study
abroad, teaching and research abroad, assistance to foreign
nations, and collaboration on the study of world problems. In
five of the six cases I have given evidence that participation is
increasing and I have concluded that, on balance, each has
tended to develop accommodative attitudes among peoples.
The effects of other forms of transnational participation—
residence abroad for business reasons, in foreign missions, and
in military service in an allied country—have not been clearly
positive for the visitors and have probably been negative for
the citizens of the host country.[24] In *Peace on the March*, however, I concluded that the total transnational balance sheet
shows gain rather than loss.[25]

It is not enough to know that the balance of effects is positive
and that participation is increasing. A third and crucial question is, How influential are the participants on the policy-
makers in their own governments? The evidence I have
scrutinized indicates that the participants in the six types having positive effects tend to be persons of above average status
in their own countries; they are, therefore, likely to have more
than average influence on legislators.[26] This is especially true
of members of INGOs, those teaching or researching abroad,
and members of technical assistance teams, though it also

seems to hold for those who visit relatives and friends, for students abroad, and for assistance volunteers. In a nutshell, transnational participation involves many who can influence government policies and it probably leads them to urge an accommodative stance toward other nations. This generalization is thought to hold both for persons who go to foreign countries and, perhaps, for the natives who come in contact with them there.

To this point we have seen participation as having a positive impact through its tendency to create trust across borders among influential citizens. We now come to another kind of facilitation, one that involves value convergence rather than personal friendships. Are nations coming to see the good world in more and more similar terms? If they are, the chances of world order are much improved, since competing religious values and economic and political ideologies have been important sources of international conflict.

It is very difficult to find measures of value convergence. Values are abstract and internal, not concrete and objective. One needs external indicators of attachment to values in order to judge whether there is convergence. Before applying to values my measure of convergence, I decided to evaluate that measure in a field where convergence is already well documented. Since the early nineteenth century we have known that industrialization tends to produce similarities in scientific and technical culture. The measure I wanted to use was the spread of particular INGOs. If the converging effects of industrialization were reflected in an increasingly similar complement of scientific and technical INGOs in nations, then this measure could be used to test for convergence of values. This would be using INGOs for a completely different purpose than that for which they were used earlier in this chapter. Then they were seen as groups within which friendships across borders developed and trust was created. Now they are simply indicators of a process of cultural convergence.

To carry out the trial I compared the INGO data in the 1964–65 *Yearbook of International Organizations* with those in the 1974–75 edition in five categories: trade unions; economics, finance; commerce, industry; technology; and science. These seemed appropriate because they are fields of human endeavor closely tied to industrialization.

In the *Yearbook*, the nations to which members of each INGO belong are classified under five heads: Europe, America, Asia, Australasia, and Africa. For my purpose I regarded Europe, America, and Australasia as a single culture area, labeled European. Thus, there were only seven possible cultural combinations that an INGO might embody: European, Asian, or African only, European - Asian, European - African, Asian-African, and European-Asian-African. I constructed an index of cultural linkage by awarding one point for each cross-cultural link in an INGO. Thus an INGO whose membership was confined to a single cultural area received no point, one in which two cultures met received one point, and one where three cultures met, making three links, received three points. In 1964–65 there were 448 organizations in the five *Yearbook* categories chosen, but 48 of them did not show the distribution of members by area. For 1974–75 there were 715 organizations with 108 lacking the information on cultural areas. Table 7 shows the results. The convergence shown by the 55.6 percent growth in cultural linkage over a ten-year span is striking.

TABLE 7
Convergence of Scientific and Technical Culture
as Shown by INGO Memberships

Organizations Drawing from:	Number of Organizations		
	1964–65	1974–75	% Increase
One culture area	188	279	48.4
Two culture areas	77	117	51.9
Three culture areas	135	211	56.3
Index of cultural linkage	482	750	55.6

Since what we already know about industrialization leads one to expect some such figure, I concluded that the index of cultural linkage using INGOs is a good measure. I then applied the same kind of analysis to values related to world issues to see whether there was convergence there, too. This time there were no categories in the *Yearbook* that as wholes I regarded as suitable. I therefore went carefully through the INGOs included in the categories labeled: religion; international relations; law, administration; and social welfare, choosing organizations whose aims and activities reflected a concern for global order. These included INGOs related to peace, human rights, international law, disarmament, the federation of nations, support for the United Nations, and the like. There were 79 such organizations in the 1964–65 *Yearbook* and 92 in the 1974–75 listing. Nine organizations in the earlier set and 18 in the later one had no data on distribution of members by cultural areas. Table 8 shows the degree of convergence of global values in the same way that table 7 showed it for instrumental aspects of life.

TABLE 8
Convergence of Global Values
as Shown by INGO Memberships

| Organizations | Number of Memberships | | |
Drawing from:	1964–65	1974–75	% Increase
One culture area	2	2	10.0
Two culture areas	4	8	100.0
Three culture areas	25	28	12.0
Index of cultural linkage	79	92	16.5

The percentage of increase in cultural linkage in ten years is less than a third as rapid for the global values as for the more instrumental elements of culture. This was to be expected since, according to sociological theory, religious and other core values are more resistant to change than instrumental aspects of life.

The conclusion about convergence of values should not be negative, however. The almost total abolition of traditional colonialism in the world since World War II strongly testifies to convergence on the value of human political dignity. This achievement in so short a time is indeed impressive. Nor is an INGO-measured convergence of 16.5 percent in a decade by any means negligible. If humanity were finding its way toward a peaceful world one-third as fast as it is toward a technologically sophisticated world, we might all be reassured.

Relevant to the promise of cultural convergence is the theory set forth by Ali A. Mazrui in his current work, *A World Federation of Cultures: an African Perspective.*[27] He believes that gradual cultural convergence is the best hope for reaching a world community, provided that the process of convergence is not dominated by a single broad culture. If there is domination, he foresees a sense of outrage in nations of the Third World and resulting conflict. Since the people whose culture derives from Western Europe have had preponderent power for several centuries, the question thus posed is whether other cultures like those of Eastern Europe, the Middle East, the Far East, Africa, and Latin America are likely to become more influential. On this score Mazrui is mildly optimistic. He thinks other cultures may not only stand up to Western culture but may begin to counter-influence it. Many students of the world situation will be less sanguine on this point than he. Even if the process of convergence remains unbalanced, however, there is the possibility of increasing cultural integration, provided that enlightened patriotism among Western nations spreads and intensifies. We saw in chapter 5 that this is a likely development.

Although convergence of values is more significant for world order than convergence of instrumental culture, an argument that the latter also has significance is possible. Scientific and technical culture is associated with occupational roles much more clearly than are values. In these days of technology-based specialization many people, even in countries at different levels of development, find their occupational role duplicated in other cultures. Every country now has at least small cadres of engineers, scientists, business executives, bankers, and accountants. We have seen that members of the same occupation often form INGOs and come into personal contact through them. But even in the absence of common membership in organizations there seems to be some sense of fellowship with persons taking the same role, no matter where they may live. Presumably this is because one can so easily stand in the other's shoes: one knows what engages the other's attention, the problems he faces. In a broad way, a similarity of role suggests a common fate. Whether this identification is strong enough to arouse a common sense of humanity is unknown, but it is a possibility.

In this chapter we have forsaken the governmental for the nongovernmental sphere, where we have examined a number of relations that either are explanatory of accommodative attitudes among nations or facilitative of them. Of the seven topics covered, three—visiting friends and relatives, study abroad, and aid to developing countries—may not continue to increase. Convergence of cultural values will no doubt continue, but it is occurring slowly; we cannot count on it for strengthening world order in the short run. Three of the seven topics, however, have particular promise: the proliferation of international nongovernmental organizations, residence abroad for teaching and research, and the collaboration of experts in the study of world problems.

9
Call for Global Effort

We have been looking at global tendencies that may be strengthening world order. It is time to put these tendencies together, assess their joint significance, and ask what more can now be done to realize peace and justice among nations.

Perhaps the most significant finding of the present study is that several nations have already transcended old-fashioned nationalism and are exemplifying enlightened patriotism. This development contradicts the widespread belief that the character of national feeling is unchangeable. Moreover, the prospect is that a few other nations will soon be joining the pioneers. If the world were not threatened by the dire consequences of expanding populations, hunger, scarcity of energy and mineral resources, pollution, and nuclear war, humanity might be able to wait for the gradual spread of enlightened patriotism around the globe. Unfortunately the pace is likely to be too slow.

But what of the other possibilities that have been explored? Do they give promise of complementing enlightened patriotism and thereby hastening the day of a satisfactory world order? The record of the United Nations is mixed. It has disappointed the hopes of its founders in at least two respects. As pointed out in chapter 6, it has had serious bureaucratic shortcomings. Although it has carried out several successful peacekeeping operations, and although Dag Hammarskjold as

149

Secretary-General pioneered the conciliatory role of preventive diplomacy, the United Nations has been unequal to the task of resolving deep-seated national conflicts. Indeed, the most persistent of them all, that between Israel and its Arab neighbors, has been more effectively approached through traditional diplomacy than through the U.N. The thirteen-day summit conference of President Sadat of Egypt, Prime Minister Begin of Israel, and President Carter of the United States at Camp David in September, 1978, was widely acclaimed as a breakthrough after thirty years of conflict. Middle-East peace was not assured, but the failure of Egypt and Israel to meet their agreed treaty deadline of December 17, 1978, was a shocking anticlimax whose portent is obscure.

Though the United Nations has not been markedly successful in the resolution of national conflicts, it has protected the rights of weak nations, condemning encroachments of the powerful, and has organized and carried through a program of multilateral aid for them. In addition, it has fostered a world attack on several of the global problems of humanity. Finally it has provided a forum for multilateral diplomacy, thereby creating an opportunity for transnational friendships among national leaders. This intimacy may in the long run have significant influence in developing trust among nations. If the United Nations could cure some of its bureaucratic shortcomings and inspire more consensus among its members, it could become the strong influence for peace that its founders intended. Its diverse accomplishments have not yet reached that critical mass that could generate a sudden increment of public confidence and trust.

Though not designed to foster world order directly, the specialized agencies of the U.N. system were intended to make indirect contributions. Some of them, such as the World Bank, the World Health Organization, the Food and Agriculture Organization, and the International Civil Aviation Organization have clearly done so.

The regional intergovernmental organizations of consultative and technical types have made the unspectacular but useful contribution of wrestling with geographically limited tasks. They have thus freed the United Nations to wrestle with the more crucial global tasks. They have also performed a quite different service—that of encouraging enlightened patriotism by proving to their nation-members that international initiatives, at the regional level at least, are not only tolerable but helpful.

Opposed to these functions that support world order are the functions of the mutual security organizations. By building up armaments and fostering mutual suspicions, they detract from that order. Some say that these organizations have become like parties in national politics and are therefore contributing to the normal operation of the United Nations; but the fallacy, here, is that in the United Nations there is not the same binding loyalty that holds parties to peaceful procedures in a national arena. The mutual security organizations, in my opinion, detract from the capabilities of the United Nations.

Finally, the many transnational nongovernmental activities, organizations, and processes of the contemporary world seem to be fostering a slow trend toward greater cooperation among nations. As compared with hostile feelings preserved by the mutual security organizations, however, their impact is weak. They may be building a supranational spirit that will ultimately break through and spread enlightened patriotism around the globe, but so far that spirit is only mildly in evidence.

Two broad judgments flow from the analysis in the earlier chapters. One is that many of the hopeful developments have been unintended and are consequences of actions taken for other reasons. Enlightened patriotism, for instance, has flowed from rising levels of enlightenment, membership in international nongovernmental organizations for private reasons, and trade across national borders. Similarly, those technical and consultative regional organizations that are compatible with strengthening world order have rarely developed for that purpose. Among the few integrative agencies that were so intended, besides the U.N. itself and the specialized agencies, are the transnational networks and organizations purposely devoted to research and action on global problems. These have indeed had the aim of serving humanity and have welcomed the interest that the United Nations has taken in their work.

The second broad judgment is that world order will come slowly. The negative influence of the mutual security organizations will largely counteract the positive influences of other intergovernmental organizations and the nongovernmental ones. The prospects are that the spread of enlightened patriotism will be gradual. Narrow nationalisms will be kept alive by the Middle East animosities, the Third World resentment of the affluence of European and North American nations, and the fear on the part of weak Asian nations of Communist expansion. Not only will the bureaucratic deficiences of the United Nations yield to reform sluggishly, but that body is confronted with increasingly difficult problems in Africa as blacks in Rhodesia and South Africa demand political equality and majority rule, and as the Soviet Union and Cuba give military support to left-wing parties that are seeking to take over several governments.

The expectation that progress will be slow is discouraging, since it is urgent to reach a more stable world order *before* the problems of population, hunger, disruption of ecosystems, and competition for scarce resources get out of hand and cause nuclear war. People around the world need to be made aware of how close humanity is to serious failures in technological, biological, and human systems and how quickly the strains of the situation could escalate to produce widespread and violent conflict. They might then realize how imperative it is that a firm world order be established soon, an order based upon the abolition of nuclear weapons, declining national military forces, the development of a strong U.N. military arm, and acceptance by national governments of World Court jurisdiction in all international disputes. This realization would put priority where it needs to be—on genuine peace—so that the

other pressing problems can be tackled by the nations cooperatively.

Norman Cousins has put the matter well:

This is the time for all good men to come to the aid of
civilization, finding their way to each other across national barriers. They must not hesitate to proclaim their
allegiance to the family of man, working with the
sovereignities if possible, and against them if necessary.
The growth of such an enlightened world citizenry, backing strongly the work of a restructured UN, represents
the greatest hope for peace with justice. . . . [1]

An Indian scholar, Rajni Kothari, is somewhat more hopeful:

. . . A growing sense of world crisis [is] felt by literally
thousands of people living round the world. Some of
these occupy fairly influential positions in various
societies and include outstanding scientists, intellectuals,
administrators, and men of affairs. These men and
women are not just visionaries; they *know* that a crisis of
major proportions is brewing right in their midst and it
calls for concerted action. . . . [2]

There is no doubt that the world needs a surge of concerted
action. There is also no doubt that we cannot now prescribe
how to make the action feasible and effective. It seems clear
that the nations, as now constituted and as organized collectively in the United Nations, are not likely to show the way. Their
foreign policies are tightly controlled by goverments unused to
taking bold initiatives in global matters. It also seem clear that
no existing nongovernmental organization can become the
dynamic agency for the purpose. Each INGO has limitations of
one sort or another—a restricted membership base, ideological commitment, or an ineffective history.

It is much more likely that the dynamic element will emerge

from the stir being created by the meetings and publications of the Club of Rome, the Pugwash Conferences on Science and World Affairs, the World Order Models Project, the Council for the Study of Mankind, the Stockholm International Peace Research Institute, and similar bodies. Scientists, humanists, and statesmen are conferring and writing about world affairs at a great rate these days, and by so doing are enlightening interested citizens in many countries, stimulating some of them to become politically active.

Some students of the world situation believe that strengthening the world order should be a second priority. To them the first task is to put an end to the dominance of the industrialized nations in the world. To these critics it is a mistake to achieve a firmer world order before the distribution of power is more nearly equal between states. They fear that what they see as the present inequitable system will become further entrenched. The third report to the Club of Rome seems to agree that the removal of gross inequalities of income and economic opportunities in international life has the highest priority.[3] My own view is that it is more urgent to survive, while delaying reforms that would bring greater justice, than it is to carry out difficult reforms at the risk of nuclear holocaust.

What, then, can be done to start the surge of concerted action toward world order? What seems possible, though immensely difficult, is to create a transnational voluntary group whose special aim would be to further international accommodation in every possible way. "Lobbying" suggests a selfish interest, but lobbying for an unselfish cause is exactly what this group would do: promoting peace and world order. Such a group would have to be so large as almost to constitute a movement, since the promotion of peace-seeking policies would have to be carried on in most nations, all regional security organizations, and various bodies of the United Nations system. The group would be acting as a voluntary world fellowship in a vital cause.

Such a fellowship giving first priority to a firmer world order would of course be supported by the many organizations already active in the fields of disarmament, peace, and world amity. The International Confederation for Disarmament and Peace, the Women's International League for Peace and Freedom, and War Resisters International are a few of the many supportive groups. Though not having the same affinity with the proposed fellowship as these organizations, the many organizations interested in world problems of hunger and population, pollution, the law of the sea, and the scarcity of natural resources should also be enthusiastic. They would benefit from the increased consciousness of global interdependence that a fellowship focused on world order would foster.

It would be so difficult for so novel a fellowship to become a legitimate organization on the world scene that it would have to be launched under the most favorable auspices. There would have to be trusted sponsors, and the founding members would have to be known both in their own nation and beyond its borders as persons of breadth and stature. They could not be selected by governments because then they would simply reflect the policies that already control United Nations decisions. Autonomy is of the essence if the fellowship is to exert influence in new directions.

All in all, it would seem best for a small founding group to be selected by leaders from bodies already working to mitigate global tensions. One possibility would be for three organizations to take this initiative: the International Confederation for Disarmament and Peace, which promotes close cooperation between national and international peace organizations; the Club of Rome, which has sponsored probing studies of various aspects of the world predicament; and the Stockholm International Peace Research Institute, a nongovernmental organization with a cosmopolitan board of directors and a twelve-year history of scientific studies related mainly to disarmament. These are indeed bodies that could be trusted to undertake seriously and without bias the nomination of a founding group of fellows. Once the desired number of nominees (perhaps twenty-five to forty) had agreed to serve, the sponsoring bodies would have fulfilled their responsibility and the founding group would be left with autonomy to draw up a constitution, adopt a set of initial policies, and begin the selection of the much larger membership that would be necessary.

The nominating organizations would of course be cognizant of the need for founders from different regions of the world, different ideologies, and different races. It would seem wise to include citizens from two classes of nations. The first class comprises the "pioneers" discussed in chapter 4 and nations close behind them in potentiality for enlightened patriotism (shown in table 5). Their citizens would be welcomed as founders because of the respect and trust in which their nations are held.

The other class whose citizens would be peculiarly fitting as founders are the developing countries, even though many of them were established too recently to enjoy world trust. Developing nations tend to be suspicious of developed nations because so many of them have experienced the frustrations of colonialism. The selection of some of their leading figures as founders would reassure the Third World and give the movement added legitimacy.

Though the objective of the fellowship and the character of the nations represented in the founding group will be prime considerations in its worldwide acceptance, the personal characteristics of the founders will also carry weight. The future of the fellowship will be more promising if the nucleus contains at least a scattering of well-known and admired world figures. It seems axiomatic that few, if any, should be citizens of the United States or the Soviet Union. These nations are so widely judged to be trying to dominate the world that the presence of their citizens in the core, however devoted to the common cause, would arouse grave suspicions.

A possibly serious obstacle to the creation of a satisfactory founding group would be the refusal of governments to allow their citizens to serve. Despite measures to guarantee the impartiality and competence of the members selected, some governments might view the whole proposal as a plot to undermine their sovereignties. This would cast an ominous shadow over the whole enterprise before it was sufficiently developed to prove its worth. This dire possibility makes it absolutely essential that the nominating organizations and the founders they select be unimpeachably trustworthy.

It is perhaps presumptuous to discuss anything further before such a fellowship exists, but a brief exposition of my own ideas may serve to give a concreteness that is useful as a basis for discussion. Clearly the founders would hope to recruit intelligent and forceful volunteers, knowledgeable about world affairs and highly committed to the attainment of a firm world order soon. Once recruited, the participants, whether individuals or groups, would be expected to exert their influence at levels suited to their abilities—among their neighbors, within political parties, among officeholders and bureaucrats in local, provincial, and national governments, and in international nongovernmental and governmental organizations, including the United Nations and its specialized agencies. Wherever there are persons, groups, or organizations that affect world politics directly or indirectly, there would the members of the fellowship try to exert influence. To achieve world order over any span of years is a challenge; to achieve it before the year 2000 would be miraculous. But this is the miracle the movement would attempt to bring to pass. Its slogan might be the awkward but accurate: World Problem Solving through World Order—Soon.

A world fellowship such as sketched would be quite compatible with Richard Falk's vision of the transition from the present unsatisfactory situation to a firm world order. In *A Study of Future Worlds*, he declares that it must be an active, not a drifting, transition and that its stages will probably be the raising of consciousness about the world's problems, the mobilization of peoples to confront those problems, and the creation of global structures to solve them.[4] It is hard to imagine the successful completion of the first two stages without the impetus that would be given by such a world fellowship.

The fellowship depicted is no more than a suggestion. My aim has been to emphasize what needs to be done, not to stress details of organization and procedure. If others have superior designs and methods, so much the better. The main thing is to get more dynamism into the tentative process of developing a more livable world. Peoples must wake up and realize that humanity will soon be facing crises that can only be overcome by working together.

Any attempt to summarize a study so ramified as this one is quite impossible. Its completion has left me, however, with several conclusions. I believe that Heilbroner's gloomy predictions for the future of world order were unduly pessimistic (though I suspect he meant to shock his readers out of their lethargy). My research suggests that hope, slender as it may be, does exist. There are encouraging processes at work here and there. It seems to me just possible that a vigorous promotional fellowship could add strength and cohesion to these processes and save the day before world problems plunge nations into devastating war. But someone must respond to the challenge, and soon.

Appendices

APPENDIX A

Allocation of Causal
Influence to the Predictors

In chapter 3 it was explained that allocation of differential causal power to the predictors was essential to the forecasting of possible changes in NSWO scores calculated in chapter 4. I made such an allocation, but I did not explain the details of the process because of its technicality. For those interested, the details are presented here.

The unique contribution of each predictor (leaving aside overlap with other predictors) is easily obtained by subtracting the coefficient of determination (the multiple correlation squared) of the four other variables from the five-variable coefficient of determination (0.470). This simply shows how much explained variance is lost when the predictor in question is omitted from the calculation. These unique contributions are shown in the second column of table 9. Their sum, 0.390, is 0.08 less than the multiple coefficient of determination of 0.470 for the five predictors. Thus the problem is how to distribute the 0.08 that is missing because of overlap. There is some guidance from the fact that the allocation cannot exceed the coefficient of determination of each variable singly with the NSWO index (which includes overlap). These coefficients are simply the squares of the correlation coefficients of each predictor with the NSWO index, given in the first column of the table.

The chief problem in making the allocations was that INGO participation and enlightenment had a correlation of 0.76 with each other, showing a large overlap that could not be scientifically distributed. I made the decision on a common sense basis to give most of the shared influence to enlightenment, on the ground that it affects a far larger proportion of the population than INGO participation and is therefore much more likely to foster the latter than INGO participation is likely to foster enlightenment. Though, as said in chapter 3, INGO participation is a more specific influence on support for world order, enlightenment is broader and perhaps more basic.

TABLE 9
Relations between Predictors and the NSWO Index

Predictors	Correlation Coefficient	Unique Contribution	Coefficient of Determination	Estimated Predictive Power
INGO participation	.56	.201	.317	.21
Enlightenment	.44	.046	.190	.11
Urgency of foreign trade	.31	.078	.097	.08
Productivity relative to reference countries	.38	.059	.144	.06
Population pressure	−.15	.006	.021	.01
Total		.390		.470

Predicted Scores of 114 Nations on The Index of National Support For World Order

Rank	Nation	Score	Rank	Nation	Score
1	United States	71.97		Mexico	53.87
	Sweden	68.44			
	Luxemburg	67.90	31	Chile	53.31
	Switzerland	66.48		Ireland	53.23
	Belgium	66.11		Spain	53.02
				Romania	52.92
6	Britain	65.92		Greece	52.48
	German				
	Federal Republic	65.91	36	Bulgaria	52.19
	France	65.73		Lebanon	51.96
	Canada	65.26		Turkey	51.81
	Denmark	65.07		Brazil	51.72
				Portugal	51.28
11	Netherlands	64.77			
	Norway	62.95	41	Peru	50.60
	Iceland	62.36		South Africa	50.23
	Italy	60.60		Cuba	50.11
	Czechoslovakia	60.53		Panama	50.04
				Taiwan	49.78
16	Australia	60.44			
	Austria	60.34	46	Iran	49.57
	Kuwait	59.91		Morocco	49.25
	Finland	59.20		Ghana	49.20
	Japan	59.06		Egypt	49.11
				Philippines	48.98
21	Israel	58.74			
	New Zealard	58.61	51	Malaysia	48.70
	Argentina	58.26		India	48.47
	Soviet Union	57.33		Iraq	48.34
	Hungary	57.01		Colombia	48.21
				Tunisia	48.04
26	Poland	56.18			
	Venezuela	54.51	56	Gabon	47.97
	Yugoslavia	54.48		Costa Rica	47.79
	Uruguay	54.36		Jamaica	47.60

Rank	Nation	Score		Rank	Nation	Score
	Cyprus	47.57			Albania	44.18
	Libya	47.46			Central	
					African Republic	44.07
61	Syria	47.32			Dominican	
	Sri Lanka	47.19			Republic	44.02
	South Korea	46.88				
	Malta	46.86		91	Bolivia	43.95
	Senegal	46.52			Sudan	43.82
					Zaire	43.48
66	Saudi Arabia	46.49			Togo	43.37
	Algeria	46.29			Cambodia	43.29
	Jordan	46.22				
	Liberia	46.06		96	Mauretania	43.15
	Thailand	45.83			Mongolia	43.11
					Nepal	42.99
71	Ivory Coast	45.81			Tanzania	42.78
	Congo	45.62			Malawi	42.72
	Pakistan	45.48				
	Cameroon	45.47		101	Honduras	42.66
	Zambia	45.44			Argentina	42.61
					Guinea	42.59
76	Guatemala	45.25			Burma	42.24
	Nicaragua	45.20			Dahomey	41.99
	Ecuador	44.98				
	South Vietnam	44.89		106	Niger	41.31
80.5	Indonesia	44.75			Ethiopia	41.27
					Haiti	41.26
80.5	El Salvador	44.75			Chad	41.12
	Kenya	44.71			Mali	40.84
	Nigeria	44.58				
	Malagasay	44.51		111	Laos	40.74
	Paraguay	44.34			Somalia	39.79
					Upper Volta	39.65
86	Sierra Leone	44.31			Yemen	39.39
	Uganda	44.30				

Appendix C

Limitations on
Organizations Selected for
Studying of Bridging

The first limitation imposed on the data from the *Yearbook of International Organizations* was to omit all organizations that are part of the United Nations network. Since such organizations aspire to be universal in their memberships and do in fact usually bridge the mutual security organizations, they are not suitable for measuring differences in bridging over time. The second and more restrictive limitation excluded all intergovernmental organizations that serve a merely technical function, like regional research institutes, advisory bodies in the fields of education and culture, and organizations that facilitate cross-boundary communication and transportation. To state the matter positively, organizations were included that were judged to have impact, direct or indirect, on the general public of a nation, so that cooperation of governments in them would have some moderating effect on cleavages expressed in opposing mutual security organizations. Thus organizations for political cooperation, the promotion of trade relations, and agricultural and industrial development were included. The third limitation was to omit as redundant all bodies that were subordinate to the mutual security organizations themselves.

165

APPENDIX D

Members of Mutual Security Organizations

1964		1974

North Atlantic Treaty Organization

Belgium	Italy	Same nations
Britain	Luxemburg	
Canada	Netherlands	
Denmark	Norway	
France	Portugal	
German Federal	Turkey	
Republic	United States	
Iceland		

Central Treaty Organization

Britain	Pakistan	Same nations
Iran	Turkey	

South-East Asia Treaty Organization

Australia	Pakistan	Pakistan withdrew
Britain	Philippines	
France	Thailand	
New Zealand	United States	

Warsaw Treaty Organization

Bulgaria	Hungary	Same nations
Czechoslovakia	Poland	
German	Romania	
Democratic Republic	Soviet Union	

League of Arab States

		Added
Algeria	Morocco	Arab Emirates
Egypt	Saudi Arabia	Bahrain
Iraq	Sudan	Mauretania
Jordan	Syria	Oman
Kuwait	Tunisia	Qater
Lebanon	Yemen Republic	Somalia
Libya		Yemen Democratic
		Republic

1964		1974

Organization of African Unity

		Added
Algeria	Malawi	Botswana
Burundi	Mali	Equatorial Guinea
Cameroon	Mauretania	Gambia
Central African	Morocco	Kenya
Republic	Niger	Lesotho
Chad	Nigeria	Mauritius
Congo	Rwanda	Swaziland
Dahomey	Senegal	
Egypt	Sierra Leone	
Ethiopia	Somalia	
Gabon	Sudan	
Gambia	Tanzania	
Ghana	Togo	
Guinea	Tunisia	
Ivory Coast	Uganda	
Liberia	Upper Volta	
Libya	Zaire	
Malagasy	Zambia	

Organization of American States

		Added
Argentina	Honduras	Barbados
Bolivia	Mexico	Jamaica
Brazil	Nicaragua	Trinidad and
Chile	Panama	Togago
Colombia	Paraguay	
Costa Rica	Peru	
Dominican Republic	Salvador	
Ecuador	United States	
Guatemala	Uruguay	
Haiti	Venezuela	

Notes

Chapter 1

1. Robert L. Heilbroner, *An Inquiry into the Human Prospect* (New York: W. W. Norton & Company, Inc., 1974), chapter 2.
2. Ibid., p. 136.
3. Rachel Carson, *Silent Spring* (Boston: Houghton, Mifflin Co., 1962).
4. Dennis L. Meadows et al., *The Limits to Growth* (New York: Universe Books, 1972).
5. Richard A. Falk, *This Endangered Planet* (New York: Random House, 1971).
6. Mihajlo Mesarovic and Eduard Pestel, *Mankind at the Turning Point* (New York: E. P. Dutton & Co., Inc., Reader's Digest Press, 1974).
7. Ibid., p. 111.
8. Ibid., p. 145.
9. Ibid., p. 206.
10. Jan Tinbergen et. al., *Reshaping the International Order: a Report to the Club of Rome* (New York: E. P. Dutton & Co., 1976); and Ervin Lazlo et. al., *Goals for Mankind: a Report to the Club of Rome* (New York, E. P. Dutton & Co., 1977).
11. J. Robert Oppenheimer, "Atomic Weapons," *Proceedings of the American Philosophical Society* 90 (January 1946):9.
12. Not only is a world government unfeasible, it is considered by many humanists to be undesirable, on the ground that it would produce a world culture that would become uncreative for lack of counter stimulation.
13. David Alleo and Benjamin Rowland, *America and the World Political Economy* (Bloomington: Indiana University Press, 1973) p. 191.
14. Charles Horton Cooley, *Social Process* (New York: Charles Scribner's Sons, 1918), chapter 1.

Chapter 2

1. Gunnar Myrdal, "Peace Research and the Peace Movements," *Center* [for the Study of Democratic Institutions] *Report* 7 (June 1974):5.
2. Morris Ginsberg, *Nationalism: a Reappraisal* (Leeds: Leeds University Press, 1961), pp. 26-27.

Chapter 3

1. Another approach would have been to obtain data on national support for world order at two times, separated by ten years, and collect information on changes in conditions in the meantime that might explain changes in support.
2. Robert Cooley Angell, "National Support for World Order: a Research Report," *Journal of Conflict Resolution* 17 (September 1973):429–54.
3. Bilateral aid to developing nations is not included in this indicator. Unlike multilateral aid through United Nations agencies, bilateral aid cannot be assumed to be supportive of world order. It may be given to obtain support in a prospective war.
4. The data on size of delegations to the United Nations are the average for the years 1961–66 as reported in Robert Keohane, "Who Cares about the General Assembly?" *International Organization* 23 (February 1969):141–49. The data on bilateral diplomatic representation are for 1963–64 as reported in Chadwick Alger and Steven Brams, "Patterns of Representation in National Capitals and Intergovernmental Organizations," *World Politics* 19 (July 1967):646–63.
5. The data for this indicator were kindly supplied by Peter H. Rohn from the United Nations Treaty Project directed by him at the University of Washington.
6. The data were gathered by the World Event/Interaction Survey, conducted under the supervision of Charles A. McClelland at the University of Southern California.
7. The five intergovernmental organizations are the International Bureau of Education, the International Committee of Military Medicine and Pharmacy (which supports professional collaboration in the spirit of the Geneva Convention), the International Office of Epizootics (which promotes research on the pathology and prophylaxis of contagious diseases), the International Union for the Publication of Customs Tariffs, and the Permanent Court of International Justice.

8. Robert Cooley Angell, *Peace on the March: Transnational Participation* (New York: Van Nostrand Reinhold, 1969). The original title was "The Creeping Vine of Peace," a title more descriptive of its contents than the title adopted by the publisher.
9. Karl W. Deutsch, *Nationalism and Social Communication: an Inquiry into the Foundations of Nationality* (Cambridge, Mass.: M. I. T. Press, 1953), p. 126.
10. Angell, *Peace on the March*, chapter 9.
11. Robert Cooley Angell, *The Moral Integration of American Cities* (Chicago: University of Chicago Press, 1951), p. 16.

Chapter 4

1. William Bross Lloyd, *Waging Peace: The Swiss Experience* (Washington, D.C.: Public Affairs Press, 1958), p. 72.
2. Armin Gretler and Pierre-Emeric Mandl, *Values, Trends and Alternatives in Swiss Society: a Prospective Analysis* (New York: Praeger Publishers, 1973), p. 214.
3. Edgar Bonjour, *Swiss Neutrality: its History and Meaning* (London: George Allen and Unwin, 1946), pp. 126–27.
4. Stanley V. Anderson, *The Nordic Council: A Study of Scandinavian Regionalism* (Seattle: University of Washington Press, 1967), p. 124, quoting Tage Erlander at the eighth session of the Nordic Council.
5. Ibid., p. 149.
6. Marquis W. Childs: *Sweden: The Middle Way* (New Haven: Yale University Press, 1956).
7. Torsten Nilsson, "The Foreign Policy of Sweden," *American-Scandinavian Review* 53 (March 1965): 15–19.
8. Helge Hveem, *International Relations and World Images: A Study of Norwegian Foreign Policy Elites* (Oslo: Universitetsforlaget, 1972).
9. Ibid., p. 129, table 4.6.2.
10. Mari Holmboe Ruge, "Small Power vs. Big Power Perspective in Foreign Policy," *Proceedings of the 3rd IPRA Conference* (Assen: Van Gorcum Co., 1970), pp. 203–13.
11. Ingrid Eide Galtung, "Attitudes to Technical Assistance: A Study Based on Norwegian Public Research Data," *Proceedings of the International Peace Research Association.* Second Conference, volume 2 (Assen: Van Gorcum Co., 1968), p. 352.
12. Helge Hveem, "Foreign Policy Thinking in the Elite and the egeneral Population," *Journal of Peace Research* 5 (1968): 161, table 12.

172   *Notes*

13. Galtung, "Attitudes to Technical Assistance," p. 357.
14. Ibid., p. 361.
15. Hveem, *International Relations*, p. 171, table 5.4.14.
16. Ibid., pp. 174–80.
17. Ibid.
18. Hans Zetterberg, "Sweden—a Land of Tomorrow," in Ingemar Wizelius, *Sweden in the Sixties* (Stockholm: Alquist and Wiksell, 1967), p. 14.
19. Ibid.
20. Carleton J. H. Hayes, *Essays on Nationalism* (New York: Macmillan Company, 1926), p. 201.
21. Charles Horton Cooley, *Human Nature and the Social Order*, 2nd ed. (New York: Charles Scribner's Sons, 1922), p. 210.
22. Gustav Ichheiser, "Misunderstandings in International Relations," *American Sociological Review* 16 (June 1951): 311–16.
23. Arnold Wolfers, *Discord and Collaboration* (Baltimore: Johns Hopkins University Press, 1964), p. 6.
24. Klaus Knorr, "Transnational Phenomena and the Future of the Nation-State," in *The Search for World Order*, eds. Albert Lepawsky, Edward H. Buehring, and Harold D. Lasswell (New York: Appleton-Century-Crofts, 1971) pp. 405–6.
25. This may explain why Cutright's Index of Representation (which measures the degree of democracy in a state and which I tested as a predictor in my study of national support for world order) correlated only moderately with the NSWO index. The number of paternalistic or authoritarian governments supporting world order was perhaps sufficient to hold the correlation down to 0.47. For Cutright's index see: Phillips Cutright, "Political Structure, Economic Development, and National Security Programs," *American Journal of Sociology* 70 (March 1965) :537–50.

Chapter 5

1. The predicted scores for all 114 nations are given in appendix B.
2. The reference for Cutright's index is given in note twenty-five of chapter 4. Cutright's scale runs from four (fully democratic system) to zero (fully authoritatian system). In table 4, I have reduced the normally calculated scores on potentiality for enlightened patriotism of the following eight nations by subtracting 10 percent of the amount of overachievement for every point they fall below full democracy on the Cutright index: Brazil, Egypt, Iran, Ivory Coast, Lebanon, Liberia, Morocco, and Pakis-

tan. Since Morocco lost 3.5 of the possible four points of the Cutright index, for example, its overachievement was reduced by 35 percent, yielding a corrected potential score of 51.02 instead of 52.27.
3. F. C. S. Northrop, *The Meeting of East and West* (New York: Macmillan Company, 1946).

Chapter 6

1. Chadwick F. Alger, "Personal Contact in Intergovernmental Organizations," in Herbert Kelman, *International Behavior: A Socio-Psychological Analysis* (New York: Holt, Rinehart and Winston, 1965), chapter 14.
2. Ibid., pp. 541–42.
3. Ibid. p. 542.
4. Ibid.
5. Ibid. p. 432.
6. Ibid. pp. 527–32.
7. Ibid. p. 532.
8. Ibid., pp. 545–46.
9. Larry L. Fabian, *Soldiers without Enemies: Preparing the U.N. for Peacekeeping* (Washington, D.C.: Brookings Institution, 1970), p. 91.
10. Lester R. Brown, *World without Borders* (New York: Random House, 1972), p. 249.
11. Edward Thomas Rowe, "Strengthening the United Nations: A Study of the Evolution of Member State Commitments," *Sage Professional Papers in International Studies:* 02–031.
12. Karl Nandrup Dahl, "The Role of ILO Standards in the Global Integration Process," *Journal of Peace Research* 5 (1968) :309–51.
13. The definitive work on the ILO's development to 1963 is Ernst B. Haas, *Beyond the Nation-State: Functionalism and International Organization* (Stanford: Stanford University Press, 1964).
14. Juergen Dedring, *Recent Advances in Peace and Conflict Research* (Beverly Hills: Sage Publications, 1976) is an admirable review of the field written by a staff member of the United Nations Institute for Training and Research (UNITAR).
15. Committee for Coordination of National Research in Demography, *Directory of Demographic Research Centers* (Paris: 1974).
16. Daniel S. Cheever, "The Third Law of the Sea Conference— Treaty Law or Customary Law?" *International Studies Notes* 2 (Winter 1975): 23.

17. Jan Tinbergen et al., *Reshaping the International Order: a Report to the Club of Rome* (New York: E. P. Dutton & Co., 1976), p. 171.
18. Boyce Rensberger, "U.N. Parleys: Their Value? Conference on Deserts Raises Questions Anew," *New York Times*, Sept. 13, 1977, p. 6.
19. Ibid.
20. Brown, *World Without Borders*, pp. 214–15.
21. The literature on multinational corporations is large and rapidly expanding. For a recent and critical view of the multinationals, see Richard Barnet and Ronald Miller, *Global Reach* (New York: Simon and Schuster, 1974).

Chapter 7

1. George Orwell, *1984* (New York: Harcourt, Brace and Co., 1949).
2. Ernst B. Haas, "Regional Integration and National Policy," *International Conciliation* 513 (September 1957): 472.
3. Edward Alsworth Ross, *Principles of Sociology* (New York: Century Co., 1923), p. 164.
4. Ibid., p. 165.
5. Ibid.
6. Robin M. Williams, Jr., *American Society*, 2nd ed. (New York: Alfred A. Knopf, 1960), p. 561.
7. See appendix B for lists of the members of these seven organizations in 1974. One of them, the South-East Asia Treaty Organization, has since been dissolved.
8. John Higham, "Another American Dilemma," *Center* [for the Study of Democratic Institutions] *Magazine* 7 (July/August 1974): 72.

Chapter 8

1. Robert Cooley Angell, *Peace on the March: Transnational Participation* (New York: Van Nostrand Reinhold, 1969).
2. Chapter 9 of *Peace on the March* gives more detail on the effects of INGO participation.
3. Nils Peter Gleditsch, "Interaction Patterns in the Middle East," *Cooperation and Conflict* 1 (1971): 15–30.
4. Angell, *Peace on the March*, p. 39.

5. Franklin D. Scott, *The American Experience of Swedish Students: Retrospect and Aftermath* (Minneapolis: University of Minnesota Press, 1956), p. 101.
6. Angell, *Peace on the March*, pp. 40–41.
7. C. Robert Pace, *The Junior Year in France* (Syracuse: Syracuse University Press, 1959), p. 67.
8. Ralph L. Beals and Norman D. Humphrey, *No Frontier in Learning* (Minneapolis: University of Minnesota Press, 1957), p. 114.
9. Richard D. Lambert and Marvin Bressler, *Indian Students on an American Campus* (Minneapolis: University of Minnesota Press, 1957).
10. ———, "The Sensitive Area Complex: A Contribution to the Theory of Culture Contact," *American Journal of Sociology* 60 (May 1955): 583–92.
11. Angell, *Peace on the March*, p. 43.
12. John and Ruth Hill Useem, *The Western-Educated Man in India: A Study in his Social Roles and Influence* (New York: Dryden Press, 1955).
13. Angell, *Peace on the March* , pp. 43–44.
14. Robert H. Shaffer and Lee R. Dowling, "Foreign Students and their American Student Friends," mimeographed (Bloomington: Indiana University).
15. Angell, *Peace on the March*, p. 47.
16. For more details, see Angell, *Peace on the March*, pp. 53–54.
17. John T. and Jeanne G. Gullahorn, "Visting Fulbright Professors as Agents of Cultural Communication," *Sociology and Social Research* 46 (April 1962): 281–93.
18. C. Wendell King and Edwin D. Driver, "Report on a Retrieval Study of the Professional Person Overseas," mimeographed (Amherst: University of Massachusetts).
19. Harold Isaacs, *Emergent Americans: A Report on "Crossroads Africa"* (New York: John Day Co., 1961).
20. Brent Ashabranner, *A Moment in History: the First Ten Years of the Peace Corps* (Garden City, N.Y.: Doubleday and Co., 1971).
21. Ibid., p. 208.
22. Ibid., p. 361.
23. The four volumes sponsored by the World Order Models Project are: Richard A. Falk, *A Study of Future Worlds* (New York: Free Press, 1975), Rajni Kathari, *Footsteps into the Future: Diagnosis of the Present World and a Design for an Alternative* (New York: Free Press, 1971), Ali A. Mazrui, *A World Federation of Cultures: an African Perspective* (New York: Free Press, 1976), and Johan Galtung, *The True Worlds* (forthcoming).

24. Angell, *Peace on the March*, chapters 6, 7, and 8.
25. Ibid., chapter 11.
26. See Angell, *Peace on the March*, pp. 180–83 where I give data from James N. Rosenau, *National Leadership and Foreign Policy: a Case Study in the Mobilization of Public Support* (Princeton: Princeton University press, 1963).
27. Ali. A. Mazrui, *A World Federation of Cultures: an African Perspective* (New York: Free Press, 1976).

Chapter 9

1. Norman Cousins, "The Fault Lies in Ourselves," *Vista* 6 (January 1971) :15.
2. Rajni Kothari, *Footsteps into the Future: Diagnosis of the Present World and a Design for an Alternative* (New York: Free Press, 1971), p. 97.
3. Jan Tinbergen et. al., *Reshaping the International Order: a Report to the Club of Rome* (New York: E. P. Dutton & Co., 1976), p. 176.
4. Richard A. Falk, *A Study of Future Worlds* (New York: Free Press, 1975), chapter 5.

Index

Accommodation among nations, 137, 148, 154
African nations, 147
  north African, 60
  sub-Saharan, 60, 95, 121
Alger, Chadwick, 81-82
Algerian Rebels, 77
Allende Gossens, President Salvador, 74
American society, 117
Americas, the, 81
Andean Development Corporation, 75
ANZUS (Australia, New Zealand, United States), 72
Arab-Israeli struggle, 50, 75, 76, 77, 114, 129
Arab League. *See* League of Arab States
Armaments, 1
Ashabrenner, Brent, 139-40
Australia, 60, 72, 78
Austria, 68-69, 78, 80, 84, 85
  and Hungarian refugees, 69

Balance of power among European states, 1. *See also* Peace
Bangladesh, 95
Beals, Ralph L., 133, 135
Begin, Prime Minister Menachem, 150

Belgium, 35, 61, 78, 80
Benelux, 61
Bernadotte, Count Folke, 50
Best, Gary, 81-82
Birth Control, 98
Bolivia, 75
Brazil, 73, 85
  recent history of, 74
Bressler, Marvin, 133, 134, 135
Bridging (of cleavages between nations), 120-24
Britain, 35, 60, 62, 64-65, 77, 78, 80, 87
British Commonwealth, 64, 72
Burundi, 18

Camp David summit conference, 150
Canada, 60, 66, 67-68, 78, 85
Carson, Rachel, 2
Carter, President James, 125, 150
Castro, Prime Minister Fidel, 114
Central Treaty Organization (CENTO), 122
Charter of Economic Rights and Duties of States, 104
Chiang Kai-Shek, 88
Chile, 73, 74
China (before 1949), 84
China, Republic of (after 1949). *See* Taiwan

China, People's Republic of, 18, 70, 73, 78, 117
  relations with Soviet Union, 87
Club of Rome, 2, 3, 4, 141-42, 154, 155
  systems theory in studies by, 142
Cold War, 1, 44, 63, 85, 87, 88, 117
Collective security, 84, 116
Colombia, 73, 75
Colonialism, traditional, 147
COMECON. *See* Council for Mutual Economic Assistance
Committee for International Coordination of National Research in Demography, 96
Common Market. *See* European Economic Community
Communist bloc, 1, 21, 63, 70, 76, 84, 87, 116, 119
Communist expansion, fears of, 152
Communist nations, 29
Communist satellites, 14, 42, 44, 70
Convergence, cultural, 127, 147
  in national values, 144, 145-47
  in instrumental culture, 144-45, 146, 147-148
Cooley, Charles Horton, 7, 8, 52
Cooperation among nations, 3, 4, 7, 22, 45, 74, 99, 151
Council for the Study of Mankind, 154
Council for Mutual Economic Assistance (CEMA, formerly COMECON), 70, 71, 114
Council of Europe, 36, 42, 70
Cousins, Norman, 153
Cuba, 152

Cuban missile crisis, 114
Cultural (ethnic) minorities, 11, 125
Cutright Index of Representation, 59
Cyprus, 85, 129
Czechoslovakia, 41, 45, 69, 84

decolonization, 1, 87, 91
de Gaulle, General Charles, 65-66
Denmark, 21-22, 33, 43, 57, 80, 86
  foreign policy of, 48-49
  history of, 38-41, 47-48
detente between United States and Soviet Union, 1, 88
Deutsch, Karl W., 24
Developed nations, 4, 21, 22, 66, 89, 104, 105, 106, 107, 110, 133
  dominance of, 154
Developing nations, 4, 6, 14, 21, 103-5, 133, 147-48, 152, 155
  aid to, 36, 49, 66, 75, 87, 89, 91
  bilateral assistance to, 42, 44, 48, 61, 137, 140
  multilateral assistance to, 42-43, 44, 48, 137, 140
Diplomacy
  multilateral, 81, 115, 150
  preventive, 85, 150
  traditional, 1, 6, 88, 150
Disarmament, 1, 5, 7, 41-42, 44, 48, 49, 53, 73, 86-87
  United Nations treaties relating to, 86-87
  See also Strategic Arms Limitation Treaty (SALT)

Earthwatch, 99

East Germany. *See* Germany, German Democratic Republic
East-West cleavage among nations, 78, 118
Echeverria Alvarez, President Luis, 73
Ecuador, 75
Education, contribution of UNESCO, to world, 92
Egypt, 77, 150
Endangered Planet, This, 2
Enlightened patriotism, 51-56, 57-58, 111, 125, 147, 149, 151, 152
  potentiality for, 58 ff., 77, 78, 80, 149
Environment, problems of, 106. *See also* International Conference on the Human Environment; United Nations Council for Environmental Programs
Essay on the Principle of Population, An, 94
Ethiopia, 84, 95
European nations, 153
  cooperation between eastern and western, 42, 48, 62, 69, 72
  eastern, 147
  western, 21, 60, 80, 147
European Economic Community (EEC), 36, 42, 48, 80, 111, 114, 128
European Free Trade Association (EFTA), 36, 42, 48, 128

Falk, Richard A., 2, 157
Far eastern nations, 147
Fellowship, proposed transnational, 154, 158
  founding group, 155-57
  members of, 157
  sponsors of, 155-56
Finland, 40, 68, 69, 70, 78, 80, 86
Food and Agriculture Organization (FAO), 92, 96, 104, 150
France, 35, 60, 65-66, 77, 80, 130
Freedom of association, 91
Frei Montalvo, President Educardo, 74
Futures, 143

Galtung, Johan, 24
General Agreement on Tariffs and Trade (GATT), 90, 103
Germany, 14, 15, 84
  Democratic Republic of, 18, 63, 64
  Federal Republic of, 62-64, 78, 80
  future possibilities, 63-64
Ginsberg, Morris, 14
Greece, 61
Global problems, 1-2, 4, 5, 23, 99
  collaboration of experts in study of, 143-44, 148, 150, 152
  conferences on. *See* United Nations, conferences
Goals for Mankind, 4
Great Britain. *See* Britain
Great Powers, 41, 73, 78, 84

Haas, Ernst, 115
Hammarskjold, Secretary-General Dag, 41, 50, 85, 149
Hassan II, King Mohammad, 77
Hayes, Carleton J. H., 52

Heilbroner, Robert E. 1, 57,
    158
Higham, John, 124-25
Hitler, 14, 39, 63
Houghouet-Boigny, President
    Felix, 77
Human rights, 91, 106
Humphrey, Norman D., 133,
    135
Hungary, 41, 60, 68, 71-72
    history of, 71
Hunger, problem of, in world,
    97-98, 142, 149. *See also*
    World Food Conference
Hveem, Helge, 45-47

Iceland, 66, 68, 78
India, 60, 85, 129
Indiana University, 135
Indochina. *See* Vietnam, Re-
    public of
Indonesia, 60, 85
Industrialized nations. *See* De-
    veloped nations, 159
*Inquiry into the Human Prospect,
    An*, 1
International Bank for Recon-
    struction and Development,
    90, 103, 150
International Civil Aviation
    Organization, 90, 150
International Confederation for
    Disarmament and Peace,
    155
International Conference on the
    Human Environment, 42,
    99
    Action Plan for the Human
    Environment, 99, 100
    Council on the Human
    Environment, 100
    World Environment Day, 100

International Court of Justice
    (World Court), 110, 152
International Development
    Agency (IDA), 90, 103
International Finance Corpora-
    tion (IFC), 90, 103
International governmental or-
    ganizations (IGOs), 22, 35,
    62, 113
    crisscrossing of, 118-20
    See also Bridging
International Labour Organiza-
    tion, 21, 35, 90, 91
    United States withdrawal
    from, 91
International Maritime Consulta-
    tive Organization, 90
International Monetary Fund
    (IMF), 90, 103
International nongovernmental
    organizations (INGOs), 22,
    24, 29, 35, 37, 62, 106,
    127, 128, 129, 148, 151,
    152
    devoted to research on global
    problems, 106-7
    membership in, as measure of
    value convergence, 144
International nongovernmental
    relations, web of, 125, 127-
    48, 151
    among scientists and scholars,
    142-43
International Planned Parent-
    hood, 97
*International Relations and
    World Images*, 45
International Telecommunica-
    tions Union, 35, 90
International Union for the
    Scientific Study of Popula-
    tion, 97

International Union of Associations, 127

Iran, 76

Iraq, 60, 76

Ireland, 68, 69-70, 78, 85

Iron Curtain, 117

Israel, 60, 77, 121, 129, 150. *See also* Arab-Israeli struggle

Italy, 14, 65, 78, 80, 84

Ivory Coast, 77

Jacobson, Max, 69

Japan, 14, 60, 72-73, 78, 84, 111

Jordan, 130

Journal of Peace Research, 45

Justice, sense of, among nations, 4, 154

Kashmir, 85

Kekkonen, President Urho, 69

Kennedy, President John, 138

King, Alexander, 3, 141

Knorr, Klaus, 53-54

Korea, People's Republic of, 18, 41, 84

Korea, Republic of, 41, 84

Kothari, Rajni, 153

Kuwait, 60, 75, 78

Lambert, Richard D., 133, 134, 135

Latin American Free Trade Association, 60, 75

Latin American nations, 60, 67, 147

Law of the sea. *See* United Nations Third Conference on the Law of the Sea

League of Arab States, 121, 122, 129

League of Nations, 21, 35, 36, 39, 50, 61, 66, 72, 74, 84, 87, 90

Lebanon, 77

Liberia, 77

Lie, Trygvie, 39, 50

Limits to Growth, The, 2, 142

Luxemburg, 61-62, 78, 80

Malthus, Thomas Robert, 94

Mankind at the Turning Point, 2, 3

Marshall Plan, 66, 87

Mauretania, 77

Mazrui, Ali A., 147

Meeting of East and West, The, 73

Mesarovic, Mihajlo, 2

Mexico, 73, 106

Middle East nations, 41, 60, 85, 111, 147, 150, 152

Middle powers, 85

Migration from Europe to western hemisphere, 130

Milieu goals, 54

Military expenditures, world, 88

Military forces, declining, 152

A Moment in History: the First Ten Years of the Peace Corps, 139-40

Mongolia, 18

Morocco, 77

Multinational corporations, 107-10, 120

and supranational control, 110

as harbingers of a new world order, 109-10

Mutual security organizations. *See* Regional intergovernmental organizations, for mutual security

Myrdal, Alva, 42
Myrdal, Gunnar, 9-10

Nansen, Fridtjof, 50
Nation, 11-14, 15
  nation-states, 6, 12-13
  state-nations, 12-14
National sovereignty, 5
National support for world order,
  15-32, 51, 55, 58, 78, 79,
  127, 129
  index of, 18-23, 26-28, 31-
  32, 58
  indicators of, 16, 17-18,
  26-28
  overachievers in, 58, 60, 76,
  77
  predictors of, 23-31, 58
  underachievers in, 60, 61, 66,
  67, 75
Nationalism, 3, 4, 9-14, 30, 51-
  55, 66, 84, 152
  and homgeneity of population, 32
  future possibilities in
  Germany, 63-64
*Nationalism and Social Com-
  munication*, 24
Nationality, 10-12, 52, 55
Natural resources, shortages of,
  110, 111, 142, 149
Nehru, Prime Minister
  Jawaharlal, 87
Neocolonialism, 4, 42, 140
Netherlands, 6-62, 78, 80
Neutrality, 33-34, 35, 36-37,
  38-39, 50, 69
New economic order, 87. *See
  also* United Nations General
  Assembly, Special Session
  on a New Economic Order
New York Times, The, 17, 106

1984, 115
Nobel Peace Prize, 69
Nonaligned bloc, 70, 87
North American nations, 153
Nordic Council, 22, 40, 48, 69
Nordic nations, 85
North Atlantic Treaty Organiza-
  tion (NATO), 21, 39, 40,
  41, 44, 48, 61-67, 85-86,
  114, 116, 121-22
North Korea *See* Korea, People's
  Republic of
North-South cleavage, 119
Northeast Atlantic Fisheries
  Commission, 120-21
Northrop, F. C. S., 73
Norway, 21-22, 33, 43, 50-
  51, 75, 69, 85, 86
  foreign policy of, 44-45,
  49
  history of, 38-41, 44
  political research in, 45-47
Nuclear powers, 6
Nuclear war, 149
Nuclear weapons, 6, 116
  abolition of, 152

Operation Crossroads, 138
Organization of African Unity,
  122
Organization of American States,
  73, 74, 75, 122
Organization of Petroleum Exporting Countries (OPEC),
  76, 110
Orwell, George, 115
Overseas empires, breakup of,
  116-17

Pace, C. Robert, 132
Pakistan, 77, 85
Pan-European cooperation, 36

Patriotism. *See* Enlightened patriotism
Peace, 84, 92, 150
  commitment to the cause of, 22, 73
  need of concerted action for, 153-54
  promotion of, 154
  through balance of power, 22
Peace corps, 44, 46, 135, 138-140
Peace on the March, 128, 129, 139, 141, 143
Peace research, 93
Peace Research Institute, Oslo, 45
Pearson, Lester, 67
Peccei, Aurelio, 3, 142
Peru, 75
Pestel, Eduard, 2
Philippines, 60
Pinochet Ugarte, General Augusto, 74
Pioneers in national support for world order, 33, 38, 49, 50, 51, 53, 58, 76, 78, 80, 111, 156
Poland, 44
Pollution, 99, 100, 142, 149
Population explosion, 94
Population problem, 94-95, 142, 149. *See also* World Population Conference
Portugal, 117
Project Camelot, 137
Pugwash Conferences on Science and World Affairs, 141, 154

Red Cross, International Committee of, 18, 21, 35
Reference group analysis, 30

Regional intergovernmental organizations, 7, 113-25
  for mutual security, 113, 114-24, 151, 152
  having a consultative function, 113-14
  furthering trade, 113
  having technical functions, 113-14, 150-51
  possibilities of crisscrossing, 118-20
Rensberger, Boyce, 106
Reshaping the International Order, 4, 103
Residence abroad for teaching or research, 135-37, 148
Rhodes, Cecil, 64
Rhodesia, 18, 152
Romania, 129
Ross, Edward Alsworth, 118-19
Rowe, Edward Thomas, 90

Sadat, President Anwar, 150
Scandinavian nations, 49-50, 85
Scott, Franklin, 131
Seabed mining. *See* United Nations Third Conference on the Law of the Sea
Silent Spring, The, 2
Singapore, 18
Social scientists, attitudes toward, abroad, 136-137
South Africa, 87, 121, 152
South Asian nations, 60
South Korea. *See* Korea, Republic of
South Vietnam. *See* Vietnam, Republic of
Southeast Asia Treaty Organization (SEATO), 72, 122
Sovereignty, 6, 10, 22, 111, 157

Soviet Union, 1, 14, 39, 41, 42,
    69, 71, 73, 78, 84, 86, 87,
    90, 111, 114, 116, 122,
    152, 158
    relation with the People's
    Republic of China, 88, 117
Spain, 117
Spanish Sahara, 77
Specialized agencies. *See* United
    Nations, specialized agencies
State (national), 10-12. *See also*
    Nation; World state
Stockholm International Peace
    Research Institute, 42, 154,
    155
Strategic Arms Limitation Treaty
    (SALT), 1, 86-87, 141
Study abroad, 130-35, 148
Study of Future Worlds, A, 157
Sudan, 60
Sweden, 21-22, 33, 57, 86
    foreign policy of, 41-43, 49,
    50
    history of, 38-41
Switzerland, 17, 21-22, 50, 51,
    57
    confederation, 33-35
    federal state, 35-38, 51
    pluralistic political structure
    37-38

Taiwan, 88, 130
Tentative process, 7, 15, 113,
    117
Thailand, 60
Third world. *See* Developing na-
    tions
Tight bipolar system, 116
Tito, Marshal, 70, 71, 87
Transnational participation, 29,
    127, 129, 135, 137, 140,
    141, 143-44
Treaty of peace between Israel
    and Egypt, 150
Trinidad and Tobago, 18
Trust among nations, 150
Turkey, 61

UNESCO Statistical Yearbook,
    130
United Kingdom. *See* Britain
United Nations, 1, 5, 6, 7, 16-17,
    22, 35, 39, 43, 49, 57, 61,
    81-111, 114, 116, 149,
    150, 151, 153
    and regional organizations,
    115
    bureaucratic deficiencies of,
    87, 149, 150, 152
    Charter, 84, 115
    conferences on global prob-
    lems, 93-94, 106
    Development Program
    (UNDP), 48, 67
    Economic and Social Council
    (ECOSOC), 89, 90
    expenditures of, 89
    Fund for Population Activ-
    ities, 96
    General Assembly, 62, 69,
    75, 81, 85, 86-87, 92, 100,
    103, 119
        Conference on Interna-
        tional Economic Cooper-
        ation and Development,
        105
        Special Session on a New
        Economic Order,
        104
        Special Session on Dis-
        armament, 86
    Military arm for, 152

national commitment to, 90

peacekeeping operations, 41, 44, 48, 49, 61, 65, 67, 68, 69, 70, 71, 72, 74, 77, 85, 149

Population Commission, 97

secretary-general of, 89

Security Council, 41, 64, 69, 74, 85, 88, 115-16

specialized agencies, 5, 16, 35, 36, 44, 48, 64, 67, 68, 71, 72, 73, 77, 89, 90, 150, 152

United States role in, 66

United Nations Conference on the Law of Treaties, 68

United Nations Conference on the Peaceful Uses of Outer Space, 68

United Nations Conference on Trade and Development (UNCTAD), 103-5

United Nations Council for Environmental Programs. *See* International Conference on the Human Environment

United Nations Educational, Scientific and Cultural Organization (UNESCO), 92-93

European Coordinating Center for Social Sciences, 68

United Nations Industrial Development Organization (UNIDO), 68, 104

United Nations Population Commission, 97

United Nations Third Conference on the Law of the Sea, 100-103, 110

Law of the Sea Convention, 101, 103

Law of the Sea Tribunal, 102-3

International Seabed Authority, 102

United Nations University, 93

United States, 1, 35, 60, 66-67, 68, 73, 78, 79, 82, 86, 87, 88, 90, 111, 114, 116, 117, 119, 122, 130, 156

and Vietnam, 117

attitude toward People's Republic of China, 87

Conress of, 81

Department of State, 136

Fulbright program, 136

Peace Corps, 75

monopoly of atomic weapons until 1948, 87

Universal Postal Union, 35, 90

Universal state. *See* world state

University of Massachusetts, 136

University of Oslo, Institute of Social Research, 45

Useem, John and Ruth Hill, 134

Value changes, necessity of, 4

Venezuela, 60, 73, 74-75

Versailles, Treaty of, 14

Vietnam, Democratic Republic of, 18, 86

Vietnam, Republic of, 86, 117

Vietnam war, 66, 88

Visiting relatives and friends abroad, 129-30, 148

Voluntary work abroad, 137

Coordinating Committee for International Voluntary Work Camps, 138

Voluntary work abroad *(continued)*
  Service Civil International, 137

Waldheim, Secretary-General Kurt, 69
War Resisters International, 155
Warsaw Pact (Organization), 68, 71, 85, 114, 116, 122
West Germany. *See* Germany, German Federal Republic
West Irian, 77
Western bloc, 1, 70, 75, 87, 116, 119
Wolfers, Arnold, 53
Women's International League for Peace and Freedom, 155
World Bank. *See* International Bank for Reconstruction and Development
World Federation of Cultures: an African Perspective, 147
World Food Conference, 96, 97-99
World Health Organization (WHO), 90, 91-92, 150

World Meteorological Organization, 35, 90
World Order, 1, 6, 7, 8, 78, 81, 85, 91, 100, 111, 113, 114, 118, 120, 125, 137, 149, 150, 152, 154
  See also National support for world order
World Order Models Project, 142-43, 154
World Population Plan Conference, 96-99, 106
  World Population Plan of Action, 97
World problems. *See* Global problems
World state, 6, 7
World War I, 1, 14, 35, 52, 84
World War II, 1, 14, 35, 45, 50, 62, 70, 84

Yearbook of International Organizations, 17, 23-24, 97, 113, 121, 127, 129, 144-46
Yugoslavia, 68, 70, 85

Zaire, 85
Zetterberg, Hans, 49-50